PASSENGER LISTS
FROM IRELAND

by

J. Dominick Hackett
and
Charles Montague Early

Excerpted from

JOURNAL OF THE
AMERICAN IRISH HISTORICAL SOCIETY

Volumes 28 and 29

CLEARFIELD

Excerpted and reprinted from
Journal of the American Irish Historical Society
Volumes 28 and 29
New York, 1929-1931

Reprinted by
Genealogical Publishing Co., Inc.
Baltimore, Maryland
1965, 1973, 1977, 1981

Library of Congress Catalogue Card Number 65-29279

Reprinted for
Clearfield Company by
Genealogical Publishing Company
Baltimore, Maryland
1992, 1992, 1998, 2010

ISBN 978-0-8063-0166-2

Made in the United States of America

TABLE OF CONTENTS

PASSENGER LISTS PUBLISHED IN
"THE SHAMROCK OR IRISH CHRONICLE," 1811

J. Dominick Hackett

The date of arrival of early immigrant ancestors from Ireland in America must always be a matter of interest to descendants. The evidence of this lies in the frequent searches of such records.

Official passenger lists may be found at the port of entry. Those in New York date only from 1820 and have to be consulted, if at all, at the Custom House. These lists, which are numerous even in early days, are chronologically arranged and it is almost impossible to find an individual name unless the exact date of arrival is known because the surnames are not alphabetically arranged. The lists are incomplete even after 1820. Alphabetical lists of names of passengers previous to that time are scarce and those which have been compiled form an important source of information.

Early periodicals, such as "The Shamrock" of New York, have published lists of passengers arriving in New York and other American ports of entry from time to time and some of them have been published by our Society in "The Recorder." On account of their unique character, it has been thought desirable to publish the surnames of those who arrived in 1811 in a single alphabetical list. Unfortunately one issue of the Shamrock, July 27, is missing but it may not have contained a Passenger List. Each surname in this consolidated list is preceded by a number which identifies the ship in which the passenger arrived. "List of Ships" shows the name of each ship with its corresponding number, together with attendant particulars such as sailing and/or arrival date, place of departure and/or port of entry; thus, the number 18 preceding the entry "18 Doherty, Henry" refers to the ship, particulars about which will be found in the "List of Ships" following the list of names.

All surnames have been copied exactly as they have originally appeared except in a few cases where the facts have been ascertained or where there is an obvious typographical error. There are indications that names were taken orally from passengers by per-

sons indifferently acquainted with the Irish names or their usual
anglicized form, hence the spelling is sometimes unusual; Coil for
Coyle, Ceyrin for Kieran. Some of the names are rare, such as
Vimmo, Amberson, Turkenton, M'Knott, Charbowell, Cobine,
Clothard, Coslarder, Dettart. Others are well known in America
today such as Glass, Copeland, Roulstone, Robert Service,
Crothers, and Harding. As usual Doherty is spelled in a variety of
ways and we find Camble, Cambell and Campbell. Moreover, cer-
tain spellings tend to be stereotyped. With a few exceptions the
"M' " affix is used rather than the correct form "Mac" or its
abbreviation, "Mc". All names in the alphabetical list with the
"M' " prefix are arranged as if they had a "Mac" prefix.

The passenger lists already published in "The Recorder" have
excited interest. Several persons have been enabled to find the
time when their ancestors came to America, the place of departure
and the port of entry. For instance, Mr. John R. Morron, Presi-
dent of the Atlas Cement Company, has found that his ancestor,
John Morron of Ballybay, Co. Monaghan, departed from Belfast,
Ireland, on the "Protection" and arrived in New York in 1811.
Further, it has been possible to supply Mr. J. Keresey, New York,
with the names of his grand-parents and their kin who came from
Lismore, Co. Waterford, and sailed from Cork on the ship
"Radius" which arrived in New York May, 1811; the names, how-
ever, were written "Kearcey."

The descendants of the 2,000 individuals listed in 1811 prob-
ably number no less than 150,000 persons today. It is evident,
therefore, that the publication of the list should be of wide interest.

The small proportion of South of Ireland surnames is ex-
plained by an interesting historical circumstance. The "Belisarius,"
sailing from Dublin in 1811, was met by the British ship of war
"Atalanta" on the west border of George's Bank, and sixty-two
men, women and children, were taken off, it being alleged they
had not passed the customs. A passenger, however, claimed that
the lists were correct. He further said that those taken off were
addressed by the sailors of the British ship, "Come along; you
shan't go into that damned Republican country; we are going to
have a slap at them one of these days and you shan't be there to
fight against us."

Thus, 1811 could not be accounted a normal year of Irish immigration. In any case it is impossible to say whether all the ships

which arrived in that year are included. Moreover, some of the entries specify children, the number of which is not mentioned. It is also known that some Irish came from English ports. For instance, of 117 passengers leaving London between Dec. 11 and December 18th, 1773, Patrick Reiley, William Morgan, William Boyle, Arch. O'Brian and Thomas Gorman are all mentioned as having an Irish residence, while Terence MacDonald, James Demsay and Thomas McKoin are mentioned as having a London residence. Thus, about 7 per cent of these passengers were Irish.

In 1802 Robert Slade, secretary of the Irish Society, made a report to the governors entitled "Narrative of a Journey to the North of Ireland in the year 1802," from which the following is extracted:

"The road from Down Hill to Coleraine goes through the best part of the Clothworker's portion, which was held by the Right Honorable Richard Jackson, who was the Society's general agent. It is commonly reported in the country that, having been obliged to raise the rents of his tenants very considerably in consequence of the large fine he had to pay, it produced an almost total emigration among them to America, and that they formed a principal part of the undisciplined body which brought about the surrender of the British Army at Saratoga. I think it right to add that Mr. Jackson was considered a man of the greatest honour and integrity, and that his memory is highly respected by all who knew him."

Long before this period, however, passengers were coming from Ireland in large numbers. Cheesman A. Herrick, in his valuable book, *White Servitude in Pennsylvania,* says that, in 1729, there was received in the colony a total immigration of 6,208, of whom 267 were English and Welsh passengers and servants, 43 were Scotch servants, 1,155 were Irish, 4,500 chiefly Irish were landed at New Castle and 243 were Palatine passengers. Out of the known emigrants from Great Britain and Ireland it will be seen that over 75 per cent were Irish at this early period!

The report of the American Historial Association, 1896, quotes Phineas Bond as saying, in 1788, "I have not yet been able to obtain any account of the number of Irish passengers brought hither for any given series of years before the war—but from my own recollection I know the number was great and I have been told that in one year above 6,000 Irish were landed at Philadelphia, Wilmington and New Castle upon Delaware."

A LIST OF PASSENGERS FROM IRELAND, ARRIVING IN AMERICAN PORTS, 1811

TRANSCRIBED FROM THE "SHAMROCK" AND ALPHABETICALLY ARRANGED

NOTE: The number preceding the surname indicates the name of the ship; see "List of Ships" following.

A

21 Adams, Charles.
12 Aiken, Anne; Dromore.
12 Aiken, Jane; Dromore.
14 Aikens, John.
14 Akin, Joseph.
14 Akin, Margaret.
14 Akin, Mary.
14 Akin, William.
19 Alchorn, Michael, Philadelphia.
26 Alcorn, Francis and wife.
26 Alcorn, James.
26 Alcorn, John and family.
26 Alcorn, Joseph.
13 Alexander, Marg.
30 Alges, John.
3 Alsop, Nathaniel and wife; Seafield.
7 Amberson, James; Hill Hall.
31 Anderson, Ann.
9 Anderson, Catherine; Banbridge.
2 Anderson, George, Newtownards.
31 Anderson, Hugh.
10 Anderson, James.
26 Anderson, James.
31 Anderson, James.
2 Anderson, Jennet; Newtownards.
2 Anderson, Samuel; Newtownards.
2 Anderson, T.; Newtownards.
9 Anderson, William; Banbridge.
21 Anderson, William.
16 Andrews, Gabriel.
5 Andrews, John; Cumber.
32 Androhan, John; Wexford.
21 Anthony, William.
30 Arenner, Bernard.
18 Armitage, John; Tipperary.
25 Armstrong, Alex.
12 Armstrong, Arabella; Down.
25 Armstrong, Arm.
34 Armstrong, Eliz.
7 Armstrong, Eliza; Co. Down.
11 Armstrong, Isaac.
20 Armstrong, John.
11 Armstrong, Marg. and child.
34 Armstrong, R.
7 Armstrong, Wm.; Co. Down.
12 Armstrong, Wm.; Down.
12 Armstrong, Wm.; Down.
26 Arthur, James.
2 Aslein, John; Belfast.
30 Atcheson, Hugh and wife.
13 Atkins, Mary.
28 Atkinson, Eliza; Dromore.

28 Atkinson, Henry; Dromore.
28 Atkinson, Henry; Dromore.
28 Atkinson, James; Dromore.
28 Atkinson, Jane; Dromore.
2 Auld, James; Grange, Antrim.
2 Auld Mary; Grange, Antrim.
34, Auld, Margaret.

B

29 Bacon, John and family.
26 Bailey, Esther.
17 Baimbrick, Martin and family.
11 Ballah, William.
5 Banecan, Christopher; Ballytrea.
11 Barker, John.
34 Barklie, L., and family.
21 Barns, William.
13 Barney Patrick.
27 Barr, John and family; Ballinahinch.
28 Barron, John P.; New York.
6 Barry, James; Watergrasshill.
6 Barry, James; Youghal.
1 Barry, John; Co. Louth.
7 Beatty, Alex., and family; Hillsboro.
16 Beatty, George.
16 Beatty, Jane.
30 Beatty, Oliver.
16 Beatty, Wm.
2 Bell, David; Loughgall, Armagh.
5 Bell, David; Lisburn.
13 Bell, Jacob.
11 Bell, James.
5 Bell, James; Lisburn.
35 Bell, John.
5 Bell, Margaret; Lisburn.
13 Bell, Mary.
35 Bell, William.
27 Bennet, James; Co. Armagh.
37 Bennet, Patrick, and family.
16 Bennett, Z.
9 Best, George; Banbridge.
22 Best, John and family.
9 Best, Seragh; Banbridge.
17 Bird, Mary.
17 Bird, Thomas.
17 Birk, Eliza.
17 Birk, John.
21 Birns, Barney.
1 Bishop, John and wife; Co. Dublin.
33 Black, Donaldson, and family; Co. Tyrone.
35 Black, George.
34 Blair, Ann.

31 Blair, Catherine.
31 Blair, Eliza.
28 Blair, Eliza; Cullybackey.
31 Blair, George.
31 Blair, James.
31 Blair, Jane.
31 Blair, John.
34 Blair, Richard.
28 Blair, Samuel; Cullybackey.
31 Blair, Wm.
6 Blake, John; Emly.
12 Blany, Eleanor; Down.
1 Bleakly, William; Dublin.
20 Blythe, Keziah.
12 Bodd, James; Loughbrickland.
33 Boggs, Paul; New York.
7 Bonnel, John; Queens Co.
28 Booney, Harriet; Greencastle.
28 Booney, Samuel; Greencastle.
28 Booney, Sarah; Greencastle.
27 Bowen, Miss Susanna; Belfast.
1 Bowles, Mrs. H.; Co. Sligo.
31 Boyd, Ellen.
14 Boyd, John.
9 Boyd, John; Down.
31 Boyd, Mary-Ann.
31 Boyd, Samuel.
11 Boyd, William and family.
28 Boyd, William; Killeybegs.
21 Boyle, Catherine.
13 Boyle, Dennis.
21 Boyle, John.
30 Boyle, John.
22 Boyle, Neil and family.
21 Boyle, Terance.
36 Bradley, Cath.
36 Bradley, Francis.
19 Bradley, John; Tipperary.
10 Brady, James, and family.
18 Branigan, Thomas; Co. Louth.
28 Bridge, Anthony; Bedford, Pa.
12 Bridget, Joseph, and family, Beleek.
21 Brogan, John.
33 Brown, Alex., and family; Aughan-
    werry.
16 Brown, Ann.
20 Brown, David, and family.
2 Brown, Francis; Kelbroughts, Antrim.
3 Brown, Geo., wife and 7 children;
    Banbridge.
5 Brown, Henry; Lisburn.
8 Brown, James.
2 Brown, John; Loughgall, Antrim.
35 Brown, John, and family.
5 Brown, Rachel; Lisburn.
8 Brown, William.
31 Browne, Bridget.
31 Browne, Mary.
31 Browne, Patrick.
30 Bryan, Anne.
30 Bryan, James, and wife.
5 Bryans, Sarah; Moy.
27 Bryson, Mrs.; Belfast.
25 Buchanan, Wm.
12 Buchanon, John; Carrickfergus.
6 Buckley, Catherine; Cloinmel.
36 Buden, James, and family
6 Bull, John; Kilkenny.
31 Bull, Mary.
6 Bullen, Henry; Clonakilty.
6 Bullen, Mary; Clonakilty.
5 Bunham, Ann; Newry.
12 Burk, Robert; Down.
13 Burnes, James.
13 Burns, Catherine.
13 Burns, Darby.
10 Burns, Elizabeth.

13 Burns, Henry.
13 Burns, James.
13 Burns, Murphy
7 Burns, Samuel; Halls Mill.
13 Burns, John, and family.
13 Burns, Thomas, and family.
10 Burns, William.
35 Burns, William, and family
17 Burton, Ally.
1 Butler, Mary; Co. Wexford.
1 Butler, Michael; Co. Wexford.
18 Byrne, James; Wicklow.
19 Byrne, Miles, and family; Dublin.
1 Byrnes, Bridget; Co. Louth.
1 Byrnes, C. Jr.; Co. Louth.
1 Byrnes, John; Co. Louth.
1 Byrnes, Nicholas; Co. Louth.

C

19 Caffray, Edward; Queens Co.
13 Caldwell, John, and family.
36 Caldwell, Joseph.
23 Callaghan, Michael; Killarney.
6 Callihan, John; Tallow.
12 Calvin, Thomas; Rathfriland.
28 Cambell, Robert; Kilinchy.
9 Camble, Joseph; Duncannon.
16 Campbell, Antho.
25 Campbell, Jane.
28 Campbell, Jemimah; Belfast.
8 Campbell, John.
28 Campbell, Mary; Belfast.
36 Campbell, Patrick, and family.
2 Campbell, Mrs. W.; Blaris, Co. Down.
35 Campbell, Wm., and family.
30 Cane, Charles, and family.
29 Cannon, —, and family.
10 Cannon, John.
13 Cannon, John.
14 Cannon, Patrick.
18 Carden, N., and family; Tipperary.
6 Carey, Richard; Cork.
15 Carney, Richard; Downpatrick.
13 Carling, Philip.
7 Carlton, A.; Hillsboro.
26 Carolan, Rose.
30 Carr, Alexander.
3 Carr, John; Hillsboro
22 Carr, Joseph.
27 Carrall, Dennis; Co. Tyrone.
19 Carrall, John; Tipperary.
8 Carrigan, James.
8 Carrigan, Wm.
5 Carse, William; Killinchy.
14 Carson, George.
14 Carson, James.
14 Carson, John.
33 Cartan, Patrick, and family; Claudy.
11 Carver, Agnes.
6 Casey, John; Emly.
35 Casey, Peter.
22 Cassely, Patrick.
21 Cassidy, Francis.
33 Catherwood, Hugh; Coleraine.
6 Cavanagh, Michael; Cappoquin.
16 Ceyrin, Wm.
9 Chaley, William; Antrim.
17 Charowell, James.
31 Chestnut, Samuel.
36 Child, Alexander.
8 Christie, Margaret, and child.
12 Clagher, Jane; Armagh.
16 Clark, Ann.
16 Clark, David.
18 Clark, Edward; Cavan.

9 Clark, John; Lurgan.
14 Clark, Mary.
14 Clark, Nancy.
11 Clark, William.
16 Clark, William.
16 Clary, John.
35 Class, John, and family.
12 Cleland, John; Lisburn.
9 Cleland, Samuel; Dunleery.
5 Clement, William; Ballybay.
28 Clothard, Anthony; Killinchy.
2 Coal, Alley; Drumbo, Down.
34 Coal, Catherine, and family.
2 Coal, James; Drumbo, Down.
14 Cobine, George.
14 Cobine, Robert.
7 Coborn, Wm., and family; Kilwarlin.
20 Cochlin, James.
33 Cochran, Mr., Ballymoney.
31 Cochran, John.
3 Cochrane, Henry; Co. Mayo.
3 Cochrane, Robert; Co. Mayo.
3 Cochrane, William; Co. Mayo.
29 Coe,—, and sister.
2 Coil, Peter; Derryloran.
2 Coil, Rosa; Derryloran.
2 Coil, Sarah, Derryloran.
2 Coil, William, Derryloran.
7 Coin, Ann and children; Belfast.
19 Colin, Henry; Co. Louth.
14 Collins, Andrew.
36 Collins, James.
31 Colvin, James.
31 Colvin, John.
9 Conaghy, Barnard; Banbridge.
5 Conaghy, Thomas; Antrim.
18 Concannon, Patrick; Kilkenny.
35 Conden, Hannah, and family.
21 Conn, Jane.
21 Conn, Robert.
21 Conn, Samuel.
21 Conn, Sarah.
21 Connel, Stephen.
16 Connelly, Patrick.
17 Connor, Jane, and family.
3 Connor, James; Lisburn.
6 Connor, Jeremiah; Cork.
6 Connor, Mary; Cork.
34 Conolly, Polly, and family.
9 Cook, Henry; Armagh.
31 Cooney, Bryan.
32 Cooper, Mrs.; Dublin.
11 Copeland, James.
11 Copeland, Thomas.
7 Copeland, Wm., and family; Co. Down.
19 Corcoran, Thomas; Dublin.
19 Corcoran, Wm.; Dublin.
15 Corney, Richard; Downpatrick.
30 Corrins, James.
14 Coslarger, James.
17 Costagan, James.
35 Couden, Hannah, and family.
33 Coulter, Ann; Derry.
33 Coulter, Hugh; Pettigo.
33 Coulter, Sarah; Co. Derry.
2 Couples, Elizabeth; Aghaderg.
2 Couples, James; Aghaderg.
17 Courtney, Peter.
12 Cowser, Eliza; Armagh.
12 Cowser, James; Monaghan.
12 Cowser, Sophia, Armagh.
31 Coyle, Daniel.
31 Coyle, John.
18 Craig, Chas., and family; Dublin.
18 Craig, John.
18 Craig, Jos., and family; Dublin.
16 Craig, Wm.
33 Crampsier, John; Magilligar.

37 Cranfin, Mary, and family.
11 Crary, Samuel.
8 Crawford, Rebecca.
26 Crocket, George.
26 Crocket, Samuel.
26 Crockett, George.
26 Crockett, John.
26 Crockett, Robert.
13 Crone, William.
6 Cronin, Stephen; Castlemartyr.
21 Crosier, Eliza.
26 Cross, Elizabeth.
16 Crossen, Cornelius.
16 Crosson, Patrick.
35 Crothers, Hugh.
25 Crow, Jane.
25 Crow, Margaret.
25 Crow, William.
30 Crozier, Eliza.
30 Crozier, Richard.
21 Crummer, Ann.
21 Crummer, Cathar.
21 Crummer, Letitia.
21 Crummer, Mary.
21 Crummer, Nathl.
21 Crummer, Saml.
28 Cubbert, Isaac; Armagh.
26 Culbert, George.
18 Cullin, John; Kilkenny.
31 Cullin, James.
16 Cummings, John.
33 Cummings, John; Ballymoney.
13 Cunningham, C.
13 Cunningham, Coudy.
13 Cunningham, Dan.
6 Cunningham, Frances; Cappoquin.
12 Cunningham, Hugh; Rathfriland.
1 Cunningham, J; Sligo.
13 Cunningham, J.
6 Cunningham, John; Cappoquin.
35 Cunningham, Robert, and family.
16 Curragan, Sarah.
17 Current, Lawrence.
8 Curry, Conell.
22 Curry, John.
20 Currie, Josias.
7 Curry, Mary; Hillsboro.

D

7 Dail, Edward and family, Rathfriland.
37 Dander, Sarah.
4 Danwoody, John; Belfast.
4 Danwoody, Wm.; Belfast.
2 Davidson, John; Loughgall, Armagh.
35 Davidson, John, and family.
16 Davis, Barnard.
3 Davis, Charles; Armagh.
2 Davis, William; Blaris, Down.
15 Davis, William; Coleraine.
2 Davis, William; Hillsboro, Down.
10 Davison, John, and family.
18 Davis, Thomas; Wicklow.
28 Davis, Thomas; Armagh.
19 Daye, Andrew; Queens Co.
18 Dealy, John; Wexford.
7 Deek, Agnes; Ballynahinch.
7 Deek, James, Ballynahinch.
11 De Hart, Edward.
19 Delany, Thomas; Wexford.
8 Denvant, Michael.
9 Deolin, Arthur; Cullsalag.
9 Deolin, Daniel; Banbridge.
24 Derragh, Eliza; Kilrea.
24 Derragh, Ellen (child); Kilrea.
24 Derragh, John; Kilrea.
11 Devan, Francis.

11 Devan, Francis.
30 Dever, Edward, and family.
31 Devilt, James.
31 Devilt, Thomas.
18 Devine, Michael; Co. Louth.
36 Devlin, Sally.
20 Dick, John.
26 Dickey, James.
26 Dickey, Nathaniel.
26 Dickey, Samuel.
20 Dickson, J., and family.
22 Dickson, John.
33 Divin, Patrick; Ballyshannon.
6 Divine, William; Tallow.
14 Dixon, Mary Ann.
9 Dixon, Joanna; Dungannon.
9 Dixon, Thomas; Dungannon.
14 Dixon, Thomas.
33 Doak, David; Fannit.
2 Dobbin, Mrs.; Killeman, Down.
2 Dobbin, Leonard; Killeman, Down.
21 Dogherty, Biddy.
21 Dogherty, Cathar.
21 Dogherty, Dennis.
21 Dogherty, Edward; Carrowkeel.
21 Dogherty, George.
21 Dogherty, Isaac.
21 Dogherty, Mary.
21 Dogherty, Mary.
21 Dogherty, Philip.
14 Doholy, Edward.
14 Dolonson, Hugh, and family.
33 Donaghey, Ann; Roeman.
21 Donaghey, Barney.
21 Donaghey, Pat.
8 Donaghy, Ar.
33 Donaghy, John; Rushey.
13 Donald, Barney.
13 Donald, Eleanor.
13 Donald, Michael.
4 Donaldson, Thomas; Cupar.
8 Donell, Jane.
15 Donnell, Elizabeth; Armagh.
4 Donnelly, William; Belfast.
34 Doorish, Bernard.
16 Dougherty, Abigail.
31 Dougherty, Anthy.
31 Dougherty, Cath.
13 Dougherty, Dudly.
31 Dougherty, Henry.
8 Dougherty, James.
8 Dougherty, John.
21 Dougherty, John.
14 Dougherty, Neal.
14 Dougherty, Philip.
16 Dougherty, Thos.
14 Dougherty, William.
11 Douglass, Joseph.
16 Douglass, Joseph.
33 Douglass, Joseph; Kilrea.
5 Douglass, Robert; Ballymena.
17 Dove, Edward.
16 Doyle; Catherine.
32 Doyle, David; Dublin.
32 Doyle, Dennis; Dublin.
18 Doyle, John; Wexford.
18 Doyle, Michael; Wexford.
3 Drain, John; Co. Armagh.
3 Drain, Henry; Co. Armagh.
10 Drake, Henry.
10 Dreison; Anah.
21 Duddy, Henry.
21 Duddy, William.
1 Duffy, James; Co. Cavan.
13 Duffey, John.
1 Duffy, Fargus; Co. Monaghan.
1 Duffy, Owen; Co. Monaghan.
1 Duffy, Francis; Co. Monaghan.

17 Dunn, John.
16 Duncan, Margaret.
6 Dunnahough, Thomas; Narragh.
19 Durham, James; Dublin.
19 Durham, Margaret; Dublin.
21 Dury, John.
21 Duvas, Terance.

E

25 Eakens, Sarah.
25 Eakins, Margaret.
25 Eakins, Margaret, Jr.
25 Eakins, Rosannah.
18 Echard, George.
16 Edmondson, James.
19 Edwards, G., and family, Dublin.
22 Egar, Jane.
14 Elliot, William.
30 Elliott, Archibald, and family.
20 Emerson, Mrs., and family.
15 English, James; Downpatrick.
3 English, Robert; Scotland.
37 English, Thomas, and family.
19 Erraty, M., and family; Kilkenny.
21 Espy, Sarah.
35 Evans, Samuel.
9 Evart, David; Cullsalag.
9 Ewart, John; Moreyrea.

F

9 Fair, Ann; Saint Clair.
9 Fair, James; Saint Clair.
9 Fair, Thomas; Saint Clair.
13 Fanan, John.
13 Fanen, John.
13 Faren, Thomas.
25 Farland, Margaret.
1 Farley, Terrence; Co. Cavan.
12 Farren, Felix; Dungannon.
12 Farren, James; Dungannon.
12 Farren, Sally; Dungannon.
16 Fee, James.
16 Fee, Patrick.
3 Fendlay, Napshall; Lisburn.
15 Ferguson —; Belfast.
20 Ferguson, Hugh.
3 Ferris, Charles; Armagh.
5 Ferris, James; Banbridge.
35 Ferris, Margaret, and family.
30 Ferry, Maurice.
18 Field, John; Dublin.
16 Fife, James.
12 Finlay, John; Monaghan.
21 Finnegan, Ann.
18 Finney, Matthew; Wexford.
18 Finney, Patrick; Wexford.
1 Fitzgerald, John; Dublin.
19 Fitzgerald, Morris; Dublin.
22 Fitzimmons, Andrew.
22 Fitzsimons, John.
19 Fitzpatrick, T., and family; Cavan.
19 Fitzpatrick, Wm.; Queens Co.
16 Flanagan, Patrick.
18 Flanery, M., and family; Tipp.
35 Flanigan, John.
35 Flanigan, Patrick.
11 Fleman, Betsy.
11 Fleman, Joseph.
20 Flemming, Wm.
13 Fletcher, John.
1 Floughsby, Wm.; Dublin.
21 Floyd, John.
33 Flyn, Luke; Co. Cavan.
6 Foaley, Patrick; Lismore.

6 Fogerty, James; Dungarvan.
16 Folhall, Laurin.
17 Folly, Peter.
12 Forcade, William, and family; Belfast.
18 Forley, Patrick; Cavan.
5 Forsyth, John; Banbridge.
5 Forsyth, Mary; Banbridge.
5 Forsyth, Robert; Banbridge.
5 Forsyth, Robert; Banbridge.
5 Forsyth, Sarah; Banbridge.
5 Forsyth, Valentine; Banbridge.
14 Foster, James.
14 Foster, John.
14 Foster, John.
14 Foster, Margaret.
14 Foster, Mary.
6 Fowey, Thomas; Castlelyons.
2 Francis, Martha; Drumaul.
2 Francis, Wm.; Drumaul.
10 Frasier, James.
10 Frasier, Robert.
8 Freeborn, Thomas, and family.
34 Freeland, Wm.
6 Freeman, Samuel; Waterford.
33 Froster, Patrick; Strabane.
24 Fullam, Ann; Magherafelt.
24 Fullam, James; Magherafelt.
12 Fullan, Eliza; Lisburn.
12 Fullan, Sealton; Lisburn.
35 Fuller, Lucy.
11 Fulton, John, and family.
12 Fulton, John; Lisburn.
21 Fulton, Thomas.
8 Funston, Andrew.
1 Furlong, Edward; Co. Wexford.

G

34 Gaffin, James.
31 Gallaugher, Cath.
31 Gallaugher, Chas.
31 Gallaugher, Hugh.
31 Gallaugher, Mary.
31 Gallaugher, Mich.
31 Gallaugher, Patk.
31 Gallen, Biddy.
31 Gallen, Catherine.
31 Gallen, Hugh.
31 Gallen, James.
31 Gallen, Mary.
31 Gallen, Mary.
31 Gallen, Margaret.
31 Gallen, Owen.
31 Gallen, Owen.
31 Gallen, Sally.
9 Gallery, Eliza; Moreyrea.
9 Gallery, James; Moreyrea.
6 Gallivan, Bridget; Cappoquin.
5 Gamble, Bell; Ballybay.
5 Gamble, Eliza; Ballybay.
5 Gamble, George; Ballybay.
5 Gamble, James; Ballybay.
7 Gamble, James; Ballinahinch.
5 Gamble, John; Ballybay.
5 Gamble, Joseph; Ballybay.
9 Gamble, Samuel; Ballinahinch.
5 Gamble, William; Ballybay.
3 Garvin, Patrick; Lisburn.
21 Gatt, James.
12 Gatt, William; Dungannon.
7 Gelison, Samuel, and family; Down.
9 Gelston, James; Cumber.
16 Genagal, Mary.
31 George, Adam.
20 George, Alexander,
9 George, Andrew; Killead.

20 George, Eliza.
26 George, John.
14 George, John, and family.
35 George, John, and family.
20 George, M.
9 George, Martha; Killead.
9 George, William; Killead.
14 George, William, and family.
18 Gerighaty, Owen; Meath.
34 Getty, James.
32 Gibbons, William; of Ohio.
16 Gibson, Andrew.
22 Gibson, David.
22 Gibson, Robert.
22 Gibson, William, and family.
17 Gilbert, Ann.
17 Gilbert, John.
17 Gilbert, Joseph.
17 Gilbert, Mary Ann.
1 Giles, John; Baillieboro.
16 Gillaspie, James.
13 Giller, Jacob.
14 Gillespie, Fanny.
33 Gillespie, Francis; Ballyshannon.
14 Gillespie, Michael.
8 Gilmer, Samuel.
22 Gilloe, Alexander.
31 Gilmour, John.
14 Given, James.
14 Given, John.
14 Given, Margaret.
36 Givun, John.
22 Glasgau, John.
13 Glass, Alex.
13 Glass, Isabella.
5 Glass, James; Belfast.
9 Glass, John; Grable.
16 Glen, Samuel.
24 Glenfuld, Edward; Lisburn.
21 Glinchy, John.
13 Golley, Dominick.
5 Gordon, Easter; Banbridge.
20 Gordon, James, and family.
31 Gordon, John.
5 Gordon, William; Banbridge.
15 Gorman, Thomas, and family; Castleblaney.
11 Grabbin, Peter.
34 Grady, George, and niece.
8 Graham, Cath., and family.
17 Graham, James.
33 Graham, John; Kilrea.
28 Gray, Elizabeth; Armagh.
28 Gray, George; Armagh.
27 Gray, James; Co. Antrim.
28 Gray, Jane.
25 Gray, John.
28 Gray, Jane; Armagh.
28 Gray, John; Armagh.
28 Gray, Samuel; Armagh.
28 Gray, Walter; Armagh.
28 Gray, William; Armagh.
7 Green, Sally; Lurgan.
18 Gregory, John; Co. Louth.
18 Gregory, M., and family; Meath.
2 Grendle, Robert; Kilmore; Armagh.
2 Grendle, Sarah; Kilmore, Armagh.
8 Grey, James.
31 Griffeth, Biddy.
31 Griffeth, Rose.
31 Griffin, Daw; Fannit.
21 Griffith, Jane.
21 Griffith, Mary.
21 Griffith, Robert.
26 Grimes, James.
12 Gruir, John, and family; Belfast.
6 Guess, James; Borrisokane.

20 Guiy, Margaret.
20 Guiy, Mary.
18 Gunea, Susan; Dublin.
6 Gunn, John; Castlereagh.
7 Gurley, John, and family; Co. Down.
24 Gurry, John, and wife; nigh Downpatrick.

H

13 Hagerty, Daniel.
13 Hagerty, Michael.
13 Haggerty, Mary.
1 Hales, Thomas; Glasstown.
30 Hall, Alexander.
7 Hall, Hobert, and family; Belfast.
14 Hall, John.
30 Hall, Robert.
20 Hall, Samuel.
19 Hallugan, Richard; Co. Louth.
8 Hamard, Michael.
8 Hamill, John.
31 Hamill, John.
16 Hamilton, Charles.
9 Hamilton, Conway; Molany.
16 Hamilton, Daniel.
8 Hamilton, Edw.
9 Hamilton, Elizabeth; Molany.
8 Hamilton, John.
7 Hamilton, John; Hillsboro.
9 Hamilton, Margaret; Molany.
7 Hamilton, Mary; Hillsboro.
31 Hamilton, Robert.
5 Hamilton, Robert; Cumber.
5 Hamilton, Thomas; Antrim.
28 Hamilton, Thomas; Connors.
16 Hamilton, Wm.
8 Hanagan, Denis
31 Hanlan, John.
8 Hanlan, Margaret, and family.
29 Hannah, James, and family.
14 Hanshaw, David.
23 Harding, Charles; Cork.
17 Harding, William, and wife.
14 Harkin, Hugh.
18 Harman, Bridget; Co. Louth.
20 Harper, Catherine.
20 Harper, Jane.
20 Harper, Joseph.
20 Harper, Richard.
35 Harpur, James.
20 Harris, Mary.
20 Harris, Samuel.
28 Harris, Thomas; Banbridge.
9 Harrison, Jane; Cairn.
2 Harrison, John; Aghaderg.
2 Harrison, Mary; Aghaderg.
9 Harrison, Thomas; Cairn.
32 Harrold, James; Dublin.
21 Harshaw, John.
11 Harshaw, John, and family.
21 Harshaw, Margaret.
21 Harshaw, William.
9 Harshaw, William; Down.
20 Hartley, Wm.
14 Harver, Edward.
16 Harvey, David.
2 Harvey, Robert; Blaris, Down.
2 Harvey, Mrs.; Blaris, Down.
7 Hasby, Robert; Maze.
6 Haskett, Massy; Borrisokane.
6 Haskett, Richard; Borrisokane.
21 Haslam, Margaret.
21 Haslam, William.
33 Hasting, Elizabeth; Co. Cavan.
13 Haughey, Benjamin.
13 Haughey, Peter.

12 Hawthorn, Agnes; Ballikeel.
34 Hawthorn, David, and family.
12 Hawthorn, John; Ballikeel.
20 Hayson, Susanna.
12 Hazleton, Edward; Down.
13 Hazleton, John.
1 Hearn, Thomas; New York.
26 Hector, Robert.
33 Hemphill, John and family; Dugh
   Bridge.
10 Henderson, James, and family.
30 Henderson, John.
21 Henderson, Marg.
21 Henderson, Robert.
30 Henderson, S.
21 Henderson, William.
11 Henrietta, Frances.
11 Henrietta, Francis.
20 Henry, Augustus.
5 Henry, John; Rathfriland.
22 Henry, Michael, and family.
33 Henry, Robert; Coleraine.
13 Henry, William.
12 Heran, Martha; Loughbrickland.
12 Herker, James; Belfast.
12 Heson, William; Carmery.
11 Hetherton, Betsy.
13 Hickings, Patrick.
13 Hickings, William.
33 Hilton, John; Gawagh.
14 Hinds, John.
7 Hinds, Richard, and family; Dromore.
12 Hodgsdon, John; Down.
22 Hodgson, Thomas.
35 Holland, Henry, and family.
18 Horan, John; Kings Co.
18 Horan, John; Tipperary.
1 Horan, Simon; Mullicash.
14 Huges, John.
24 Hughes, Arthur; Belfast.
3 Hughes, Jas.; Dublin.
11 Hughes, John.
28 Hughes, John; Bangor.
3 Hughes, Peter; Ballybay.
10 Hughes, Richard, and family.
17 Huges, Robert, and family.
10 Hun, Rachel.
14 Hunter, Ann.
33 Hunter, David; Omagh.
16 Hunter, Eleanor.
31 Hunter, Gerard.
16 Hunter, James.
11 Hunter, John.
31 Hunter, John.
33 Hunter, John; Newtownlimavaddy.
31 Hunter, Martha.
31 Hunter, Mary.
26 Hunter, Moses.
14 Hunter, Robert.
33 Hunter, Robert; New York.
11 Hunter Samuel, and family.
30 Hunter, Thomas.
16 Hunter, Wm.
20 Hurley, J.
20 Hurley, Wm.
14 Hutchin, John, Jr.
33 Hutchinson, Thomas; Kilrea.
20 Hutchison, Wm.
8 Hutton, John.

I

31 Irvine, Andrew.
31 Irvine, John.
12 Irvine, Samuel and family; Dungannon.
5 Irwine, George; Waringstown.
5 Irwine, George; Waringstown.
5 Irwine, Rachel; Waringstown.

J

33 Janga, Neal; Castlefin.
33 Jack, John; Co. Antrim.
22 Jackson, Mary.
25 Jackson, John.
20 Jameson, John.
9 Jamison, Agnes; Killinchy.
9 Jamison, Samuel; Killinchy.
35 Jeffrys, John, and family.
34 Jackson, Luke.
2 Jenkinson, Mrs.; Loughwall.
2 Jenkinson, Ann; Loughgall.
2 Jenkinson, Elizabeth; Loughgall.
2 Jenkinson, Isaac; Loughgall.
2 Jenkinson, Isaac; Loughgall.
2 Jenkinson, James; Loughgall.
9 Johnson, David; Antrim.
9 Johnson, Elizabeth, Antrim.
9 Johnson, Elizabeth; Hillsboro.
9 Johnson, Elnor; Antrim.
9 Johnson, Hugh; Hillsboro.
10 Johnson, James.
9 Johnson, John; Antrim.
13 Johnson, Samuel.
33 Johnston, Francis; Pettigo.
10 Johnston, Henry, and family.
25 Johnston, John.
33 Johnston, Robert; Pettigo.
8 Jolly, Patterson.
34 Jones, John.
18 Justin, Martin; Queens Co.

K

36 Kain, Percival.
30 Kane, Charles, and family.
21 Kane, Eliza.
20 Kane, Francis, and family.
1 Keally, Patrick; Dublin.
6 Keane, Margaret; Cork.
6 Kearceay, John; Lismore.
6 Kearceay, Margaret; Lismore.
6 Kearceay, Thomas; Lismore.
9 Kearns, Elizabeth; Aghada.
9 Kearns, James; Aghada.
6 Kearney, Francis; Birr.
6 Kearney, Michael; Borrisokane.
8 Kearny, Patrick.
11 Keating, Abraham.
18 Keating, John; Dublin.
18 Keating, Mary, Dublin.
20 Keenan, Dennis.
20 Keenan, Hugh.
11 Kell, John.
33 Kelly, Catherine; Fennit.
33 Kelley, Daw; Ballintrea.
33 Kelley, John; Ballybofey.
36 Kelley, Philip.
1 Kelly, Darby; Co. Meath.
19 Kelly, Michael; Drogheda.
12 Kelly, Molly; Dungannon.
14 Kelly, Neal.
27 Kelly, Patrick; Dublin.
14 Kelly, Robert.
12 Kelly, Thomas; Dungannon.
37 Kench, Richard.
4 Kenmaer, Andrew; Broomhedge.
2 Kennedy, Mrs. J.; Donaghmore, Tyrone.
7 Kennedy, James; Halls Mill.
7 Kennedy, Rachel; Banford.
7 Kennedy, Robert; Banford.
10 Kennedy, Thomas.
29 Kennedy, William, and wife.
18 Kenney, Catherine; Dublin.
18 Kenney, Peter; Dublin.
6 Kent, Redmond; Lismore.

10 Ker, James.
31 Kerr, Allen.
8 Kerr, Catherine, and family.
13 Kirr, Daniel.
35 Kerr, James.
13 Kerr, John.
26 Kerr, John.
24 Kerr, John; nigh Kilrea.
26 Kerr, Matthew.
24 Kerr, Rachel (wife) and 4 children, nigh Kilrea.
19 Kerwan, James; Castlepollard.
19 Ketly, Matthew; Kilkenny.
31 Kevenagh, James.
16 Key, Wm.
11 Kill, John.
14 Killy, Daniel.
18 Kinch, James; Wexford.
18 Kinch, T., and family; Wexford.
17 King, James.
17 King, Jane.
17 King, Jane, and 5 children.
17 King, Mary.
17 King, Richard.
6 Kirby, Cornelius; Cork.
6 Kirby, Eliza; Cork.
6 Kirby, Mary Ann; Cork.
33 Kirk, George; Mountcharles.
25 Kirk, P.
35 Kirk, Samuel, and family.
31 Kirkpatrick, John.
8 Kirkpatrick, Math.
31 Kirkpatrick, Wm.
13 Kirr, Daniel.
36 Knox, Dean.
30 Knox, James, and family.
28 Knox, Jane; Broughshane.
28 Knox, Jane; Broughshane.
3 Knox, Joseph; Ballybay.
28 Knox, Thomas; Broughshane.
31 Knox, Wm.
28 Knox, William; Broughshane.

L

17 Lacy, Edward.
7 Lamb, John; Maze.
8 Lambert, John.
6 Lane, Ellen; Clonmel.
6 Lane, John; Clonmel.
6 Lane, Mary, Clonmel.
17 Langer, Richard.
18 Lanigan, George; Longford.
19 Laplin, John; Kilkenny.
34 Lapsy, Nicholas.
16 Larkie, Alex.
16 Larkie, Mary.
1 Larkin, Miss W.; Co. Wexford.
16 Laverty, James.
28 Laverty, Jane; Newtownards.
28 Laverty, Hugh; Newtownards.
24 Law, Wm.; Belfast.
2 Law, William; Killinchy.
18 Lawler, Patrick; Wexford.
6 Leaky, John; Glanmire.
19 Leary, Michael; Castlepollard.
34 Leman, James.
34 Leman, Margaret.
11 Lemman, George.
11 Lemman, Mary.
8 Lenon, Henry.
1 Leonard, Francis; Glasstown.
20 Leviston, Charles.
20 Leviston, James, and family.
20 Leviston, Mary.
2 Lictson, Mary; Larne, Antrim.
2 Lictson, Thomas; Larne, Antrim.

14 Lindsay, Andrew.
30 Lindsay, David.
14 Lindsay, Isabella.
30 Lindsay, James.
6 Linnen, Luke; Cappoquin.
11 Lister, Eliza, and child.
2 Liston, Eliza; Kilmore, Armagh.
2 Liston, John; Kilmore, Armagh.
10 Little, James.
14 Little, John, and family.
10 Little, Martha.
12 Lockat, John; Down.
20 Lockery, James.
20 Lockery, Margaret.
8 Logan, Charles.
12 Logan, John; Bellikiel.
10 Logan, Mary.
31 Logan, Mary.
31 Logue, Biddy.
31 Logue, James.
31 Logue, Mary.
31 Logue, Wm.
30 Long, Thomas, and family.
31 Loughead, Cath.
31 Loughead, Edward.
33 Love, James; Donaghadee.
33 Love, Robert; Donaghadee.
7 Lowry, Robert, and family; Charlemont.
18 Lucas, Betsy; Queens Co.
28 Luke, James; Antrim.
16 Lurkie, Jane.
32 Lynch, John; Navan.
20 Lynn, Daniel, and family.
8 Lyons, Cornelius.
21 Lyons, Eliza.
21 Lyons, James.
21 Lyons, John.
21 Lyons, Joseph.
21 Lyons, Mary.
8 Lyons, Peter.
13 Lyons, Robert.
21 Lyons, Samuel.

M

10 MacAllisted, Felix.
10 MacAllisted, James.
20 MacAllister, R.
20 MacAllister, Rose.
9 MacAlpin, Hugh; Molany.
9 MacAlpin, James; Molany.
9 MacAlpin, Jane; Molany.
33 MacAlvin, Alex., & family; Co. Antrim.
14 MacAnnulty, James.
12 MacAnorney, Michael; Rathfriland.
26 MacArthur, John.
26 MacArthur, Robert.
30 MacAskin, John.
9 MacAtter, Betty; Blaris.
9 MacAtter, Mark; Blaris.
9 MacAttur, Ann; Killead.
9 MacAttur, James; Killead.
27 MacBride, James, wife and family; Co. Down.
1 MacBrien, John; Glasstown.
16 MacBrine, Jane.
22 MacBurney, Mrs.
11 MacCabe, Betsy.
11 MacCabe, James.
1 MacCabe, Patrick; Co. Dublin.
31 MacCafferty, Edw.
8 MacCafferty, Susan.
8 MacCaghy, Nath., and family.
12 MacCaird, William; Monaghan.
12 MacCammar, Samuel; Armagh.
2 MacCance, James; Newtownards.
10 MacCane, Robert.

5 MacCartney, Eliza; Banbridge.
5 MacCartney, Ellen; Banbridge.
5 MacCartney, Hannah; Banbridge.
12 MacCartney, John; Loughbrickland.
12 MacCartney, Nancy; Loughbrickland.
5 MacCartney, Patrick; Banbridge.
5 MacCartney, Samuel; Banbridge.
5 MacCawlley, Hugh; Crumlin.
9 MacCarton, Charles; Ballinahinch.
9 MacCarton, James; Ballinahinch.
8 MacCaughall, Geo.
21 MacCaughan, Alex.
19 MacClane, John; Co. Cavan.
19 MacClane, Mary; Cavan.
34 MacClean, David, and family.
22 MacClenaghan, James.
26 MacCloskey, James.
20 MacCloy, Thomas, and family.
36 MacClure, Anne.
28 MacClure, Thomas; Saintfield.
30 MacColgin, John.
13 MacColley, John.
5 MacComb, Ann; Keady.
5 MacComb, Henry; Keady.
5 MacComb, Margaret; Keady.
20 MacComb, Robert, and family.
5 MacComb, Thomas; Keady.
20 MacConaghy, Alex.
13 MacConley, John.
20 MacConnaghy, Jas.
26 MacConnell, James.
7 MacConnell, James; Hill Hall.
35 MacConnell, John.
20 MacConnell, P., and family.
7 MacConnell, Sarah; Hill Hall.
35 MacConnell, John.
20 MacConnell, P., and family.
7 MacConnell, Sarah; Hill Hall.
21 MacConstand, Esther.
13 MacConway, Edw.
18 MacCormick, Thomas; Longford.
33 MacCosker, Bernard; Omagh.
9 MacCoskery, John; Down.
31 MacCoun, Charles.
21 MacCousland, Ann.
21 MacCousland, Mar.
21 MacCousland, Mary.
33 MacCoy, Joseph, and family; Florence-court.
5 MacCracken, Robert; Ballymacarret.
33 MacCready, Elinor; Gortward.
8 MacCready, John.
33 MacCready, Wm.; Gortward.
20 MacCrecan, James.
21 MacCreery, John.
31 MacCue, Daniel.
31 MacCue, Michael.
21 MacCue, Thomas.
12 MacCullaugh, John, & family; Carmery.
21 MacCulloch, Geo.
20 MacCulloch, Mary.
20 MacCulloch, Wm.
34 MacCullough, Alex.
7 MacCullough, Hamilton; Co. Tyrone.
25 MacCully, Mathew; Crumlin.
22 MacCune, Clem.
16 MacCurdy, Morgan.
16 MacCurdy, William.
7 MacCurry, Henry; Hillsboro.
12 MacCurtney, James; Loughbrickland.
33 MacDermot, Susana, & family; Derry.
36 MacDevitt, P.
11 MacDonald, Moore.
28 MacDonald, Robert; Portaferry.
17 MacDonald, William.
20 MacDonnell, James, and family.
9 MacDowl, Alexander; Ilandery.
9 MacDowl, Alexander; Saint Clair.

9 MacDowl, Elizabeth; Saint Clair.
9 MacDowl, Ezibella; Ilandery.
9 MacDowl, John; Saint Clair.
9 MacDowl, Mary Ann; Saint Clair.
9 MacDowl, Rachel; Saint Clair.
9 MacDowl, Thomas; Saint Clair.
33 MacEliver, George; Donaghdee.
8 MacElkeney, Robert
26 MacElroy, Arch., and family.
33 MacElwin, Hugh; Dromore.
3 MacElwrath, Rob't, wife and child; Hollywood.
21 MacEver, William.
19 MacEvory, John; Dublin.
30 MacEwen, John.
31 MacFaddin, Eleanor.
31 MacFaddin, Manus.
12 MacFade, Jane; Hillsboro.
13 MacFaden, John.
3 MacFall, John; Portglenone.
25 MacFarland, John, wife and family.
31 MacFarland, Wm.
30 MacFarland, Wm., and family.
14 MacFaul, Daniel.
14 MacFeely, Charles.
13 MacGanty, Edward.
33 MacGaughrin, Farguis; Donegal.
34 MacGaw, John, and family.
28 MacGaw, Robert; Stewardstown.
28 MacGaw, Thomas, Stewardstown.
16 MacGellaghan, Pat.
21 MacGill, Anthony.
8 MacGinley, Corn.
22 MacGinnis, Bernard.
13 MacGinness, Danl.
11 MacGleeve, James.
24 MacGlonan, Ann, wife; Ballymoney.
24 MacGlonan, James; Ballymoney.
24 MacGlonan, Mary; Ballymoney.
24 MacGlonan, Nathaniel; Ballymoney.
8 MacGohey, Mary.
31 MacGowan, Philip.
16 MacGrath, James.
16 MacGrath, Marg.
30 MacGrath, Patrick.
16 MacGrath, Thos.
19 MacGrath, Wm.; Drogheda.
13 MacGrave, Marg.
13 MacGreedy, John.
1 MacGuinness, Edw.; Co. Meath.
8 MacGuire, Roger.
11 MacGurrah, John, and family.
17 MacHolland, Mich.
20 MacIldoon, Hugh.
21 MacIlroy, Charles.
35 MacIndoo, Robert and wife.
16 MacIntire, Abrm.
33 MacKagh, Nancy, Castlefin.
6 MacKardy, David; Dungannon.
31 MacKay, Charles.
33 MacKee, George; Mountcharles.
20 Mackee, James.
9 MacKee, Jane; Magradill.
9 MacKee, John; Ballynahinch.
9 MacKee, John; Magradill.
5 MacKee, Margaret, Newtownards.
5 MacKee, Patrick; Armagh.
5 MacKee, Robert; Newtownards.
5 MacKee, Thomas; Newtownards.
9 MacKelery, Jane; Moneyrea.
9 MacKelery, William; Moneyrea.
35 MacKenney, Alice.
5 MacKenny, Alexander; Bangor.
2 MacKenzie, Alex., Loughgall, Armagh.
2 MacKenzie, John; Newtownards.
2 MacKenzie, Philip; Loughgall.
2 MacKenzie, Ralph; Loughgall.

34 MacKever, Edward, and family.
35 MacKey, Daniel, and family.
6 MacKey, Ellen; Fermoy.
19 MacKey, James; Tipperary.
6 MacKey, Thomas; Fermoy.
9 MacKey, Thomas; Dunleary.
8 MacKinlay, George.
8 MacKinlay, John.
26 MacKinley, Hugh.
36 MacKinney, Eliza.
36 MacKinney, George.
16 MacKnight, Andrew.
16 MacKnight, Daniel.
16 MacKnight, David.
16 MacKnight, Jane.
16 MacKnight, Mary.
16 MacKnight, Thomas.
30 MacKnott, Robert, and family.
14 MacKosker, Hugh.
2 MacLanna, John; Derrylonan.
8 MacLary, Benjamin.
8 MacLaughlin, Ann.
8 MacLaughlin, Benj.
31 MacLaughlin, Biddy.
31 MacLaughlin, Elea.
11 MacLaughlin, F., and family.
31 MacLaughlin, Fran.
26 MacLaughlin, H.
8 MacLaughlin, Philip.
16 MacLeon, Patrick.
14 MacLoran, Neal.
14 MacLoran, Patrick.
16 MacLorten, Cather.
16 MacLorten, Terrence.
9 MacMagan, Agnes; Banbridge.
9 MacMagan, David; Banbridge.
9 MacMagan, Seragh; Banbridge.
7 MacMahan, Sarah; Dromore.
25 MacMahin, Rebecca.
10 MacMahon, Henry.
36 MacMalin, Wm.
1 MacMally, James; Co. Meath.
13 MacMannyman, John.
36 MacManus, Francis, and wife.
29 MacManus, Mary.
8 MacMenamy, Jos.
8 MacMennamy, Mgt.
33 MacMennomy, Edward; Ballybofey.
8 MacMenamy, Thos.
8 MacMenamy, Wm.
33 MacMinimim, Edward; Castlefin.
4 MacMullan, Hugh; Co. Down.
5 MacMullen, Eliza; Larne.
9 MacMullen, Eliza; Tyrone.
9 MacMullen, James; Tyrone.
35 MacMullen, John, and family.
9 Macmullen, Robert; Tyrone.
2 MacMurray, Alex; Kilmore, Armagh.
2 MacMurray, Hannah; Kilmore; Down.
24 MacMurray, Nancy, 2 children; nigh Kilrea.
24 MacMurray, Wm.; nigh Kilrea.
37 MacMurray, Wm.
4 MacMurrey, Mathew; Belfast.
11 MacMurry, Samuel, and tamily.
21 MacNeal, Frank.
31 MacNeal, Roger.
24 MacNeill, Neal; Belfast.
34 MacNeilly, John.
21 MacNought; James.
3 MacPeak, Owen; Portglenone.
30 MacPharland, widow and 2 children.
30 MacPharland, P.
35 MacQuaid, Edward.
15 MacQuillan, H., and family; Down-Patrick.
31 MacShane, Thomas.

11 MacSleeve, James.
26 MacTogert, Mrs., and family.
20 MacVay, M., and family.
33 MacVeagh, Patrick; Campsey.
5 MacWhatey, Jane; Armagh.
5 MacWhaty, John; Armagh.
5 MacWherter, Jane; Newry.
8 Madden, John.
20 Maffett, James.
16 Mages, Joseph.
5 Magell, Ekiza; Banbridge.
5 Magell, John; Banbridge.
5 Magell, Samuel; Banbridge.
16 Magis, Joseph.
7 Maguinis, Isabella; Co. Down.
7 Maguinis, John; Co. Down.
22 Mahaffy, James, and family.
7 Maharg, James; Co. Down.
36 Maitland, Wm.
24 Malcomson, John, Portadown.
6 Maloney, Margaret; Aglish.
6 Malowney, Jerry; Aglish.
6 Malowney, John; Aglish.
1 Malvin, William, wife, 5 sons and 4 daughters; Co. Cavan.
13 Manely, Henry.
1 Manly, Joseph; New York.
13 Manely, Michael,
12 Maney, Patrick; Rathfriland.
14 Mansfield, Robert.
31 Manson, John.
7 Mark, Joseph; Dromore.
15 Marks, John, and family; Armagh.
5 Maron, Owen; Ballytrea.
8 Marshall, Eliza.
8 Marshall, Jeorge.
8 Marshall, Joseph.
8 Marshall, W., and family.
29 Martin, —, and family.
12 Martin, Andrew; Kilmore.
28 Martin, Anna; Antrim.
26 Martin, James.
4 Martin, James; Bangor.
33 Martin, James; Newtownlimivaddy.
28 Martin, Jane; Charlemont.
33 Martin, John; Newtownlimivaddy.
26 Martin, Martha.
28 Martin, Nancy; Antrim.
26 Martin, Samuel.
20 Martin, Thomas, and family.
33 Martin, Thomas; Kilrea.
33 Masterson, Ann; Co. Cavan.
33 Masterson, Edward; Co. Cavan.
30 Mathew, Patrick.
17 Mathews; Stephen, and wife.
34 Mathews, Thomas, and family.
14 Mathewson, Wil.
10 Maxwell, Wm.
16 Maze, Francis.
14 Meehan, Catherine.
14 Meehan, Owen.
20 Meckin, Jos.
18 Meeghan, Patrick; Tipperary.
17 Menieur, Dennis.
9 Mention, Agnes; Blaris.
9 Mention, Alexander; Blaris.
9 Metchon, John; Killead.
14 Michel, Joseph.
8 Miligan, Elizabeth.
36 Miller, Anne.
14 Miller, Elizabeth.
24 Miller, Matty; Dungannon.
14 Miller, Robert.
24 Miller, Robert; Dungannon.
2 Miller, Mrs. William; Ahahill, Antrim.
16 Mills, Andrew.
13 Minetes, Biddy.

13 Minetes, Francis.
30 Moffit, John.
12 Moffit, Margaret; Armagh.
20 Molineau, James.
3 Mollin, Patrick, wife and 4 children; Armagh.
13 Mollony, John.
16 Monegan, Francis.
30 Monoghan, Torry.
2 Montgomery, J.; Counmoney, Antrim.
22 Montgomery, Joseph, and family.
4 Montgomery, Moses, wife and 3 children; Killele.
22 Montgomery, Wm., and family.
12 Moore, Eliza, Dungannon.
12 Moore, Henry; Rathfriland.
11 Moore, James.
2 Moore, James; Donaghmore, Tyrone.
35 Moore, John.
11 Moore, Margaret.
12 Moore, Mary; Rathfriland.
24 Moore, Mathew, wife and 3 children; Strabane.
36 Moore, Robert.
12 Moore, Robert; Dungannon.
12 Moore, Thomas, and family; Rathfriland.
31 Moore, William.
33 Moorhead, Samuel; Co. Antrim.
29 Moran, —, and family.
12 Morgan, James; and family; Down.
11 Morgan, Luke.
27 Morran, Andrew, and wife; Co. Down.
16 Morrison, Elizabeth.
7 Morrison, James, and family; Armagh.
7 Morrison, John; Magheragall.
16 Morrison, Martha.
5 Morron, John; Ballybay.
12 Morrow, Ellen; Monaghan.
10 Morrow, James, and family.
10 Morrow, Jane.
12 Morrow, Jane; Monaghan.
12 Morrow, Jane; Monaghan.
7 Morrow, John; Banford.
2 Mubrea, H., Newtownards.
16 Mulden, Anthony.
20 Mulholland, George.
30 Mullay, James, and family.
29 Mulony, James.
10 Munn, William, and family.
21 Murdock, M. Anne.
21 Murdock, Esther.
21 Murdock, John.
21 Murdock, John.
9 Murdough, Matthew; Moira.
1 Murphy, James; Co. Louth.
35 Murphy, John.
18 Murphy, John; Wexford.
12 Murphy, Mary; Monagher.
30 Murphy, M., and wife.
19 Murphy, Matthew; Dublin.
17 Murphy, Michael, and family.
6 Murphy, Timothy; Castlelyons.
19 Murphy, Timothy; Kings Co.
12 Murphy, William; Monagher.
6 Murry, Edmund; Aglish.
14 Murry, James.
22 Murry, James, and family.
13 Murry, Rodger.
19 Murtagh, Thomas; Drogheda.

N

17 Nailor, Wm., and family.
31 Nanson, Mathew.
1 Neall, Mathew, and wife; Co. Meath.

17 Needham, Catherine.
17 Needham, Eliza.
17 Needham, Valient.
28 Neil, Hugh; Crumlin.
32 Neil, Thomas; Dublin.
 4 Neilson, Eliza'h, and 1 child; Dromore.
26 Neilson, James.
 4 Neilson, James; Dromore.
 7 Neilson, John, and family; Co. Down.
14 Neilson, Thomas.
14 Neilson, William.
14 Neilson, Gerard.
14 Nelson, Gerard.
14 Nelson, John.
15 Nelson, John, and family; Drumduff.
14 Nelson, William.
15 Nelson, William, & family; Drumduff.
17 Newan, Thomas.
23 Nicholas, John, and family; Doneraile.
 7 Nixon, George, and family; Kilwarlin.
 7 Nixon, Mary, Kilwarlin.
16 Norris, Mary.
31 Norris, Mary.
16 Norris, Robert.
29 O'Brien, Dennis.
 6 O'Brien, Henry; Clonmel.
 1 O'Brien, James; Co. Meath.
21 O'Brien, Margaret.
21 O'Brien, Owen.
33 O'Donnell, James; Rushey.
14 O'Neal, Felix.
 8 O'Neill, John.
33 O'Neill, John; Co. Cavan.
33 O'Neill, Robert, & family; Co. Antrim.
12 O'Ray, Hugh; Belfast.
 7 Orr, John, and family; Hill Hall.
26 Orr, Joshua.
35 Orr, Mary.
25 Orr, Mathew.
26 Orr, Robert.
25 Orr, William.
 7 Orr, William, and family; Hill Hall.
10 Owens, John.
21 Owins, James.
21 Owins, Margaret.

P

20 Paine, Wm., and family.
 4 Park, David; Belfast.
 5 Parker, Catherine; Banbridge.
 6 Parker, Hugh; Cork.
10 Patterson, Ann.
12 Patterson, David, and family; Down.
 5 Patterson, Eliza; Bangor.
12 Patterson, George; Down.
12 Patterson, John; Ballykeel.
12 Patterson, Joseph; Down.
12 Patterson, Mary; Down.
31 Patterson, Samuel.
 5 Patterson, Wm.; Bangor.
 9 Patton, Edward; Grable.
 9 Patrick, Robert; Belfast.
33 Paul, Eliza; Omagh.
34 Peadon, Robert.
 7 Pepper, Edward, and family; Moyallen.
 9 Perry, Hugh; Cullsallag.
 9 Perry, Margaret; Cullsallag.
18 Phelan, Margaret; Tipperary.
17 Phelan, Patrick.
19 Phelan, Thomas; Kilkenny.
17 Phelan, William.
19 Philar, Peter; Queens Co.
 9 Phillips, Eliza; Glenary.
 9 Phillips, Thomas; Glenary.
13 Philson, Robert.

 8 Piden, James.
17 Pierce, Patrick.
12 Pierson, Jacob; Armagh.
12 Pierson, Jane; Armagh.
19 Pigott, Mark; Carlow.
 6 Pigott, Robin; Castlehyde.
 5 Pinkerton, James; Killinchy.
 4 Piper, Samuel; Menneyre.
 1 Plaus, Isabell; Co. Longtord.
19 Platt, John; Youghal.
21 Pollock, Hamill.
13 Pollock, Samuel.
13 Pollock, William.
24 Pooler, John; Armagh.
21 Porter, Ann.
21 Porter, Bell.
21 Porter, Elizabeth.
21 Porter, John.
12 Porter, John; Billamegary.
21 Porter, Thomas.
 8 Porter, William.
14 Potts, Robert, and family.
28 Preston, Thomas; Armagh.

Q

12 Quail, William, and family; Downpatrick.
27 Quale, William; Downpatrick.
26 Quigley, Martha.
34 Quin, Daniel.
28 Quin, Henry; Antrim.
34 Quin, Hugh.
28 Quin, Jane; Antrim.
28 Quin, John; Antrim.
10 Quin, John, and family.
28 Quin, Margaret; Antrim.
34 Quin, P.
14 Quin, Patrick.
26 Quinn, Charles.

R

30 Rafferty, John.
33 Rafferty, William; Garvagh.
 6 Ranighan, John; Cork.
31 Rankin, Robert.
16 Raulstone, Arch.
10 Ray, Thomas, W.
 1 Ray, William; Co. Cavan.
31 Rea, John.
36 Rea, William, and family.
20 Reed, David.
26 Reed, James.
30 Reed, Hugh.
20 Reed, Margaret.
20 Reid, Patrick.
 9 Reid, William; Cumber.
19 Reilly, Brien; Castlepollard.
34 Reilly, Mary.
34 Reilly, Thomas.
16 Rein, John.
30 Reynolds, Wm.
19 Reynolds, Wm.; Kings Co.
 9 Rhea, David; Killead.
 9 Rhea, Seragh; Killead.
 6 Rian, Thomas; Borrisokane.
30 Rice, Aily.
 8 Rice, Edward.
 6 Rice, Thomas; Cork.
 1 Rigan, Bridget; Co. Wexford.
32 Riley, Mrs.; Co. Wexford.
22 Riley, Margaret.
22 Riley, Nancy.
 4 Ritchie, Alx.; Bangor.

36 Ritchie, Eliz.
35 Roark, Mary.
1 Roberts, John; Dublin.
34 Roberts, George.
12 Roberts, George; Armagh.
20 Robeson, John.
28 Robinson, Jane; Willsborough.
28 Robinson, John; Willsborough.
28 Robinson, Mary; Willsborough.
32 Robinson, Thomas, & Mrs.; Queens Co.
28 Robinson, Thomas; Willsborough.
14 Robison, Andrew, and family.
14 Robston, James.
12 Rock, James; Armagh.
12 Rock, Mary; Armagh.
31 Rodder, Michael.
13 Rodgers, John.
13 Rodgers, Mary.
27 Rodgers, Miss Mary; Belfast.
26 Rodgers, Samuel.
16 Rogers, Nathan.
36 Rogers, Thomas, and family.
19 Rorke, Patrick; Tipperary.
16 Ross, Eleanor.
5 Ross, James; Killinchy.
16 Ross, Joseph.
30 Ross, Mary.
16 Ross, William.
3 Ross, William, wife and 4 children;
  Vernersbridge.
37 Rochford, John.
16 Roulstone, Harvey.
16 Roulstone, James.
16 Roulstone, Martha.
13 Rudder, John.
13 Rudder, Patrick.
21 Russel, John.
8 Russell, James.
10 Russell, Mary.
8 Russell, Thomas.
26 Rutherford, John.
26 Rutherford, Mary.
26 Rutherford, Sarah.
19 Ryan, David; Tipperary.
19 Ryan, James; Dublin.
19 Ryan, James; Queens Co.
1 Ryan, Mary; New Ross.
1 Ryan, Patrick; Co. Wexford.
17 Ryan, Rev. Mr.
19 Ryan, Thomas; Tipperary.
19 Ryan, William; Dublin.
18 Ryan, William; Tipperary.
35 Ryers, James, and wife.

S

6 Sadler, Hugh; Cork.
6 Sadler, Frances; Cork.
6 Sanders, James; Glanmire.
19 Scully, John; Borrisokane.
30 Scanlon, John.
20 Scott, A.
8 Scott, Alexander.
12 Scott, David; Ballikeel.
4 Scott, Henry; Cupar.
21 Scott, James.
30 Scott, James.
22 Scott, James, and family.
14 Scott, John.
12 Scott, Margaret; Ballikeel.
13 Scott, Thomas.
30 Scott, William.
19 Scully, John; Borrisokane.
11 Seave, John, and family.
5 See, Nevin; Ballybay.
15 Seed, William; Downpatrick.

11 Seeman, Thomas.
20 Service, Robert.
11 Sewere, John.
20 Shaw, John.
12 Shaw, Margaret; Billamegary.
12 Shaw, William; Billamegary.
21 Shaw, William.
13 Shawkling, James.
12 Shee, Arthur; Rathfriland.
34 Shepherd, James.
19 Sherlock, Patrick; Dublin.
10 Sherran Thomas.
22 Shields, George.
19 Shinluig, J., and family; Antrim.
36 Sieven, Tully, and family.
26 Simon, Jane.
2 Simpson, William; Loughgall.
5 Sinclaire, Ame; Banbridge.
5 Sinclaire, John; Banbridge.
5 Sinclaire, Mary; Banbridge.
19 Sinnot, Nicholas; Wicklow.
7 Sinton, Mary, and family; Moyallen.
31 Size, Bernard.
31 Size, Hannah.
6 Slattery, John; Lismore.
6 Slattery, Margaret; Cappoquin.
6 Slattery, Peter; Cappoquin.
11 Sleeman, Jane.
28 Sloan, Jane; Doagh.
8 Sloane, Martha.
13 Smiley, Alex.
13 Smiley, James.
8 Smiley, John.
31 Smiley, John.
32 Smith, Mr. Cornelius; Manoch.
11 Smith, Eliza, and family.
7 Smith, John; Ballynahinch.
7 Smith, Susan; Ballynahinch.
14 Smith, William.
26 Smyth, George.
14 Smyth, James.
5 Smyth, John; Downpatrick.
2 Spiers, Mrs. John; Donegore.
2 Spiers, James; Donegore.
24 Spratt, Hugh; Belfast.
12 Spratt, Mary; Carmery.
12 Spratt, William; Carmery.
33 Sproul, James C.; Stranorlar.
21 Sproul, John.
17 Stanhope, Henry, and wife.
19 Stanley, Wm., and family; Dublin.
10 Stark, Thomas.
13 Starr, Jeremiah.
31 Steel, Elizabeth.
8 Steel, James.
31 Steel, Joseph.
31 Steel, Sally.
9 Stephans, Elnor; Cumber.
9 Stephans, Thomas; Cumber.
9 Stephanson, John; Armagh.
19 Stephenson, Henry; Dublin.
9 Stephenson, Samuel; Killead.
33 Stevenson, Hugh; Donegal.
14 Stevenson, John.
21 Stevenson, John.
21 Stevenson, Martha.
14 Stevenson, William.
5 Sterling, James; Doagh.
5 Sterling, Robert; Doagh.
4 Stewart, Alexan.; Dunsmurry.
4 Stewart, Andrew,wife & child; Stewartstown.
34 Stewart, Benj.
13 Stewart, David.
34 Stewart, H.
14 Stewart, James.
4 Stewart, Jane, Jr.; Dunsmurry.

 4 Stewart, Jane, Sr.; Dunsmurry.
 1 Stewart, William; Belfast.
 4 Stewart, William; Dunsmurry.
34 Stewart, William.
31 Stirling, Martha.
31 Stirling, Thomas.
12 Stockdale, Jane; Downpatrick.
19 Stockdale, John; Dublin.
12 Stockdale, William; Downpatrick.
18 Stout, John; Wexford.
24 Strean, John; nigh Dromore.
 8 Strong, Chr.
 8 Strong, Hugh.
18 Sutliff, Edward; Queens Co.
18 Sutliff, Henry; Queens Co.
17 Sutton, William.
36 Swan, Thomas.
15 Sweeney, James; Londonderry.
 8 Sweeny, Connel.
 9 Sweeny, Prudence; Ballynahinch.
 9 Swenny, Patrick; Ballinahinch.
 9 Sweeny, William; Ballinahinch.
26 Syllyman, Billy; Killywaller.
28 Syllyman, John; Killywaller.

T

16 Tagart, Joseph.
 7 Tate, James; Maze.
 5 Taylor, James; Armagh.
13 Taylor, James.
 5 Taylor, Louisa; Armagh.
 5 Teas, Easter; Belfast.
 7 Tetterton, Ellen; Banford.
 7 Tetterton, Robert, & family; Banford.
 1 Thomas, John; Ballyhayes.
33 Thompson, Alex, and family; Lenck.
12 Thompson, Eliza; Down.
 7 Thompson, George; Belfast.
12 Thompson, George; Down.
10 Thompson, James.
16 Thompson, James.
12 Thompson, James; Down.
36 Thompson, John.
11 Thompson, John, and family.
20 Thompson, John, and family.
12 Thompson, John; Down.
12 Thompson, Joseph; Down.
10 Thompson, Marg't.
12 Thompson, Maria; Down.
 4 Thompson, Robert, and wife; Belfast.
 8 Thompson, Rob't.
21 Thompson, Rob't.
31 Thompson, Robert.
12 Thompson, Sarah; Down.
 8 Thompson, Wm.
34 Thompson, Wm.
36 Thompson, Wm.
19 Thompson, Wm.; Philadelphia.
33 Thompson, William; Carrick.
28 Thomson, James; Lisburn.
28 Thomson, Jane.
16 Thorne, John.
30 Timmory, Edward.
13 Timons, Isabella.
13 Timons, Timothy.
21 Tonner, Catherine.
 1 Toole, Emanuel; Dublin.
18 Toole, Peter; Dublin.
26 Torrers, Ann.
26 Torrers, Ruth.
26 Torrers, Samuel.
26 Torrers, Samuel.
20 Tracy, Hugh.
13 Traner, Bany.
19 Tranar, James; Queens Co.

19 Trevar, Patrick; Queens Co.
24 Trimble, William; nigh Armagh.
35 Triven, John, and wife.
17 Tuckerbury, Benj., and family.
 9 Turkenton, James; Dungannon.
 9 Turkenton, Jane; Dungannon.
 9 Turkenton, John; Dungannon.
17 Turner, Bartlett.
17 Turner, William.
28 Tweedy, Effy; Dromore.
22 Tweedy, Patrick, and family.

V

25 Vale, John.
25 Vale, Margaret.
 8 Vance, D.
 8 Vance, Isaac.
14 Vimmo, Charles.
14 Vimmo, Eliza.
30 Virtue, David, and family.

W

13 Waddel, Ralph.
21 Walker, Armstrong.
20 Walker, James, and family.
11 Walker, John, and family.
28 Walker, Robert J.; Galway.
23 Wall, Mr.; Clonmel.
 7 Wall, Easter, Banbridge.
 7 Wall, John, and family; Banbridge.
 4 Wallace, George; town of Antrim.
36 Wallace, Hugh.
28 Wallace, John; Bangor.
16 Wallace, Sam'l.
 1 Walsh, Miss F.; Co. Wexford.
 1 Walsh, John, (child); Co. Galway.
27 Walsh, John, and wife; Dublin.
 1 Walsh, Mary; Co. Galway.
17 Walsh, Thomas.
19 Walsh, William; Kilkenny.
 8 Ward, James.
33 Wardlaw, Elizabeth; Co. Cavan.
12 Warren, Hugh; Belfast.
12 Warren, Jane; Belfast.
16 Wason, Archer.
25 Wason, George .
16 Wason, Jane.
25 Wason, Margaret.
33 Wason, Nancy; Ray.
 1 Waters, Andrew; Co. Wexford.
21 Watson, James.
 5 Watt, James; Lisburn.
28 Watt, Jane; Castlewellan.
22 Watt, John, and family.
 5 Watt, Margaret; Banbridge.
28 Wattsher, John; Tyrone.
33 Wamb, John; Castlefin.
 1 Weapher, Ann; Rathfarnham.
 2 Welsh, John; Newtownards.
 2 Welsh, Louisa; Newtownards.
25 Weltch, H.
30 West, David.
 1 West, James; Glasstown.
30 West, William.
22 Wharton, Joseph, and family.
22 Wharton, Robert.
 4 White, Alexander; Dromore.
12 White, James; Down.
33 White, James; N'limavaddy.
13 White, John.
35 Wilkins, George.
16 Williams, George.
30 Williams, Henry.

16 Williams, Wm.
28 Williamson, Elizabeth; Saintfield.
28 Williamson, Henry; Saintfield.
28 Williamson, Jane; Saintfield.
34 Willikin, Mary, and family.
12 Willis, Margaret; Dungannon.
28 Willis, Mary Ann; Stewartstown.
28 Willis, Mathew; Stewartstown.
12 Willis, William; Down.
12 Willis, William; Dungannon.
19 Wilson, Benjamin; New York.
 4 Wilson, Elizabeth; Dunmurry.
21 Wilson, James.
26 Wilson, John.
 4 Wilson, Robert, wife and 3 children;
       Dunmurry.
21 Wilson, Thomas.
24 Winters, Edward; Portadown.
24 Winters, Mary; Portadown.
16 Wishat, Mary.
16 Wishat, Robert.
16 Wishat, Ruth.
16 Wishat, Sarah.

16 Wishat, Sarah.
 8 Witherington, A.
19 Withers, Henry; Dublin.
 1 Wogan, Christian; Co. Dublin.
16 Woods, Adam.
16 Woods, James.
21 Woods, James.
34 Wright, Ann.
19 Wright, Catherine; Cavan.
19 Wright, Eliza; Dublin.
36 Wright, James, and wife.
19 Wright, John; Dublin.
20 Wylie, Rachel.

Y

24 Young, David; nigh Charlemont.
14 Young, Fanny.
21 Young, James.
31 Young, John.
31 Young, Mary.
14 Young, William.

LIST OF SHIPS

ARRIVING IN AMERICAN PORTS, 1811

Code No.	Port of Departure	Date of Arrival 1811	Port of Entry	Name of Ship	Master	Days on Voyage	Passengers	Point of Origin
1.	Dublin	......	New York	Erin	Murphy	..	64	Residence
2.	Belfast	......	New York	Harvey Hide	Thos. Parker	77	61	Parish and county
3.	Belfast	......	New York	Hannibal		..	43	Where from
4.	Belfast	......	New York	Perseverance	Crawford	..	40	Where from
5.	Belfast	......	New York	Protection	Bearns	40	78	Residence
6.	Cork	......	New York	Radius	Clark	29	63	Nativity
7.	Belfast	......	New York	Algernon	Clark	36	55	Residence (?)
8.	Londonderry	......	New York	Westpoint	Boggs	..	79	....
9.	Belfast	......	New York	Jupiter	Wm. H. Hitchins	..	97	Residence
10.	....	May 19	New York	Orlando	Josiah Cromwell	35	37	....
11.	Newry	May 23	New York	Aeolus	Charles Henry	..	49	Nativity
12.	Belfast	Jun. 9	New York	Africa	John E. Scott	..	96	....
13.	Londonderry	......	New York	Golconda		..	84	....
14.	Londonderry	Jun. 12	Philadelphia	Alexandria	Edmund Fanning	..	85	Residence (?)
15.	Newry	Jun. 16	Philadelphia	Patty	Sawer	..	11	....
16.	Londonderry	Jun. 17	New York	Mary	Wallington	..	95	....
17.	Dublin	......	New York	Belisarius	Morgan	42	58	Residence
18.	Dublin	Jun. 2	New York	Huntress	Thomas Ronson	..	47	Late residence
19.	Dublin	......	New York	Shamrock	M'Keon	..	60	Nativity
20.	Belfast	......	New York	Hibernia	Graham	34	70	....
21.	Londonderry	Jly 4	Baltimore	Joseph and Phoebe	Plympton	..	102	....
22.	Newry	Jly 8	Philadelphia	Rising State	Stilwell	..	33	Residence
23.	Cork	Jly 14	Philadelphia	Isaac	Delano	..	4	Town
24.	Belfast	......	New York	Juno	Thompson	60	44	....
25.	Londonderry	......	New York	Ann	Alex. Howland	56	27	Residence (?)
26.	Londonderry	Aug. 31	Philadelphia	Fame	William Pollock	40	53	Residence (?)
27.	Belfast	......	New York	Maria Duplex		63	15	....
28.	....	......	New York	Protection	Bearns	54	71	....
29.	Dublin	......	New York	White Oak		44	12	....
30.	Londonderry	Oct. 21	New London	Mariner	Hookirk	48	57	....
31.	Londonderry	Oct. 31	Philadelphia	Harmony		70	104	Residence
32.	Dublin	......	New York	Erin		..	12	....
33.	Londonderry	......	New York	Westpoint	T. Holden	..	73	Residence (?)
34.	Belfast	......	New York	Hibernia	Graham	..	37	Residence
35.	Newry	......	New York	Aeolus		..	42	Residence
36.	Londonderry	......	New York	Alexander	Fanning	47	31	....
37.	Belfast	......	New York	Raleigh		..	7	....

PASSENGER LISTS

From "The Shamrock or Irish Chronicle," 1815-1816

Charles Montague Early

This Passenger List is a further installment of the series published in our annual volume XXVIII and from the same source, "The Shamrock or Irish Chronicle" (new series) for 1815-16. The first list proved to be of such wide interest that the present publication seems justified. Copies of the periodical are exceedingly rare and that in our possession is not in good condition. Official records of the sort were not kept till some years later and the names are not alphabetically arranged. This list forms a chapter in a book that has yet to be written on the extent of Irish immigration from the earliest time. In this circumstance the accumulation of evidence is highly desirable.

The Passenger List following covers about a year beginning September, 1815, and it includes about 3,150 names of persons from whom are descended perhaps 230,000 people living today.

The manner of presentation is the same as in the last list. Each name is preceded by a number which is also to be found in the "List of Ships" following the alphabetically arranged names. This number indicates the name of the ship, the date and place of departure and arrival for each individual wherever such particulars were obtainable from the periodical.

No less than seventy-two vessels are mentioned as having arrived at various American ports, mainly New York; from certain foreign ports, mainly Irish, with passengers having Irish names. The following list shows particulars:

EMBARKATION POINTS AND NUMBERS OF SAILINGS, 1815-1816.

Belfast 16	Galway 2	Londonderry.. 11
Cork 1	Halifax 2	Newry 7
Demerara ... 1	Lisbon 1	Sligo 5
Dublin 23	Liverpool 3	—
		Total 72

This list does not include all Irish persons who came to America in the specified period. The list of arrivals from Irish ports is possibly incomplete and, moreover, some Irish must have come by way of Canada and also from such ports as London, England.

Many names, not generally identified as Irish, are found in the list; some are rare even in Ireland. Curred, for instance, is an unusual Sligo name. Rochford is an old Norman name frequently found in Ireland. Strean is better known as Strawn, Stratton or Strahan; it is the name of an old Tyrconnell family. Tigut may be Tuite; Wacum, Sithgon and Wantya are unidentifiable. Record is possibly the same derivation as Ricard. Burr and Strawbridge are not uncommon in Ireland. As a contribution to family nomenclature the list presents many points of interest.

A LIST OF PASSENGERS MAINLY FROM IRELAND, ARRIVING IN AMERICAN PORTS

September 1815 to August 1816

Transcribed from "The Shamrock" and alphabetically arranged

NOTE: The number preceding the surname indicates the name of the ship as shown in the "List of Ships" following the alphabetical list.

A

32 Abercromby, James.
32 Abercromby, Robert.
23 Abbott, Thomas; Lisburn.
30 Acheson, Daniel, Sen.; Letterkenny.
30 Acheson, David, Jun., Letterkenny.
30 Acheson, Mary; Letterkenny.
40 Adair, A; Kilkeel, Co. Down.
52 Adair, Wm.
53 Adams, John.
62 Aeggs, Hugh.
8 Agnew, Deckey; Ballynuse.
68 Aikin, John; Londonderry.
27 Aldwell, Samuel.
45 Alexander, Anne.
64 Alexander, Anne Jane; Co. Armagh.
52 Alexander, E.
64 Alexander, George; Co. Armagh.
64 Alexander, Harriet; Co. Armagh.
13 Alexander, Isabella.
64 Alexander, Jane; Co. Armagh.
64 Alexander, Margaret; Co. Armagh.
64 Alexander, Mary Small; Co. Armagh.
64 Alexander, Thomas; Co. Armagh.
64 Alexander, Hugh Small; Co. Armagh.
45 Alexander, James.
64 Alexander, Robert; Co. Armagh
45 Alexander, Sarah Jane.
61 Allen, Agnes.
32 Allen, Eliz.
32 Allen, George.
51 Allen, Hannah.
51 Allen, Henry S.

32 Allen, James.
70 Allen, Jane.
32 Allen, Joseph.
32 Allen, Mary.
18 Allen, Mr,; Ireland.
51 Allen, Peter.
51 Allen, Peter H.
61 Allen, Samuel.
22 Allen,Thomas; Kings Co.
40 Amact, John; Kilkeel, Co. Down.
8 Anderson, A; Coleraine.
20 Anderson, Alexander; Lettermuck.
20 Anderson, Eliza; Lettermuck.
68 Anderson, Eliza; Londonderry.
53 Anderson, James.
20 Anderson, Jane; Lettermuck.
8 Anderson, John; Coleraine.
37 Anderson, Joseph.
30 Anderson, Margaret; Derry.
8 Anderson, Mrs.; Coleraine.
48 Anderson, William.
20 Anderson, William; Lettermuck.
20 Anderson, William; Lettermuck.
68 Anderson, William; Londonderry.
37 Anderson, William, mother & brother.
22 Andoe, James; Dublin.
25 Andrews, George.
21 Andrews, Robert.
21 Andrews, Robt. Jun.
21 Andrews, Thomas.
21 Andrews, Wm. Jun.
21 Andrews, Wm. Sen.
59 Annis, Mrs,; Dublin.
71 Arcy, Patrick D.; Ballmiobe.

23 Ardis, Alexander; Antrim.
66 Armstrong, Fanny & 4 children; Cavan.
7 Armstrong, Hugh; Drumgolen.
13 Armstrong, James.
13 Armstrong, James.
33 Armstrong, James; Port Norris.
49 Armstrong, John.
16 Armstrong, Mr. & family; Ballynahinch.
52 Armstrong, Samuel.
39 Arnold, J.
22 Arnold, James; Cavan.
2 Arnold, James; Cloghen, Co. Tipperary.
22 Arnold, William; Dublin.
68 Arthur, Joseph; Antrim.
68 Arthur, Rebecca; Antrim.
28 Ash, Cath., Castleblaney, Co. Monoghan.
22 Ashley, Daniel; Manchester, England.
26 Asple, Pierce; Dublin.
61 Atcheson, Adam.
24 Atkinson, David.
16 Atkinson, Francis; Loughgall.
24 Atkinson, Jas.
33 Auchanan, John; Port Norris.
40 Austin, Rebecca; Kilkeel, Co. Down.
40 Austin, Thomas; Kilkeel, Co. Down.

B

39 Bacon, Thomas.
50 Bailie, David.
50 Bailie, Isabella.
50 Bailie, James.
50 Bailie, John.
50 Bailie, John.
50 Bailie, Mary Anne.
50 Bailie, Robert.
54 Bailie, Thomas; Ballymote.
50 Bailie, William.
48 Baird, George.
45 Baird, Samuel.
41 Baird, Washington.
55 Baland, Thomas; Sligo.
16 Ball, James; Ballynahinch.
28 Ballagh, James; Ballybay, Co. Monoghan.
28 Ballagh, Robert; Ballybay, Co. Monaghan.
28 Ballagh, Robert E., Ballybay, Co. Monaghan.
43 Bambrick, Thomas; Kilkenny.
29 Bannin, John; Co. Killkenny.
53 Bankhead, —.
48 Banks, Thomas.
2 Bannan, Peter; Drogheda.
22 Barbadge, Thomas; Dublin.
54 Barbour, Matthew; Carney.
27 Bare, Samuel.
62 Barker, Thomas.
16 Barnett, James; Ballyagherty.
16 Barnett, James R.; Belfast.
27 Barry, James Casey.
48 Barr, John.
18 Barrow, Mr.; Dublin.
2 Barry, Edward.
48 Bayley, John.
54 Beattie, Andrew; Scotland.
62 Beatty, David.
62 Beatty, Eliza.
62 Beatty, Jas.
34 Beatty, William; Co. Fernanagh.
48 Bednard, William.
59 Beerman, Thomas; Queen's County.
16 Beggs, James; Tullyleck.

2 Behan, James; Co. Tipperary.
28 Bell, Abraham; New York.
16 Bell, David; Belfast.
7 Bell, George; Castlereagh.
50 Bell, H.
68 Bell, John; Londonderry.
28 Bell, Mary C.; Stramore, Co. Down.
28 Bell, Rebecca H.; Stramore, Co. Down.
62 Bell, Samuel.
62 Bell, Thomas.
28 Bell, Thomas C.; Stramore, Co. Down.
62 Bell, Wm.
59 Bennett, Thomas; Wexford.
72 Benningham, Eliza; Dublin.
72 Benningham, Thomas; Dublin.
22 Benton, Sam'l; Mountrath.
66 Bergin, Daniel; Queens County.
56 Bernard, Richard.
26 Berney, Ellen; Cavan.
26 Berney, Thomas; Cavan.
56 Berry, Francis.
56 Berry, Michael.
53 Beverly, Eliza; Scotland.
26 Binne, Thomas; Carlow.
14 Birk, John.
16 Black, Archibald; Rathlin.
67 Black, John; Rathlin.
44 Black, Moses.
31 Black, Peter; Ballybay, Co. Monaghan.
41 Blair, James.
13 Blair, Samuel.
50 Blair, Thomas.
8 Blame, William; Ballymena.
5 Blanchfield, Stephen; Waterford.
8 Bleakley, Jane; Drumbo.
8 Bleakley, John; Drumbo.
8 Bleakley, William; Drumbo.
6 Blood, David R.
28 Bloomfield, Saml; Belfast.
7 Boden, Hugh; Ballykeel.
45 Boggs, Alexander.
13 Bogle, Isabella.
13 Bogle, John.
13 Bogle, Samuel.
24 Bohan, Matthew.
68 Boke, Sohn; Londonderry.
39 Bolton, Margaret.
68 Bond, Alexander; Londonderry.
51 Borlridge, Josiah.
40 Borr, James; Portadown, Co. Armagh.
48 Borskin, George.
68 Botham, Isabella; Tyrone.
68 Botham, Robert; Tyrone.
66 Boyce, Anne; Wexford.
33 Boyd, Andrew; Camlagh, Co. Armagh.
62 Boyd, David.
50 Boyd, P.
27 Boyd, Robert.
62 Boyd, Samuel.
42 Boyd, Thomas; Co. Antrim.
53 Boyd, W.
30 Boyle, Chr.; Armagh.
14 Boyle, John, wife & 3 children.
13 Boyle, Robert.
49 Boyle, Samuel.
62 Bradford, James.
35 Bradley, James; Liverpool.
62 Bradley, John.
59 Bradley, John; Navan.
49 Bradley, Peter.
51 Bradley, Philip.
48 Bradley, William.
62 Bradley, Wm.
22 Brady, Anne; Cavan.
25 Brady, Hugh.
71 Brady, Hugh; Currefin, Co. Galway.

54 Canway, Catherine; Mount Temple.
54 Canway, Mary; Mount Temple.
54 Canway, Owen; Mount Temple.
68 Carabine, Catherine; Londonderry.
68 Carabine, Thomas; Londonderry.
46 Carey, Michael; Donegal.
68 Carlan, Patrick; Londonderry.
68 Carlan, Sarah; Londonderry.
26 Carle, John W., Limerick.
26 Carle, Michael; Limerick.
50 Carleton, J.
50 Carleton, J.
50 Carleton, M.
48 Carlin, James.
48 Carlin, John.
8 Carlin, Thomas; Co. Down.
16 Carlisle, James; Balinahinch.
16 Carlisle, John; Balinahinch.
68 Carmachy, Robert; Tyrone.
68 Carmeran, Allen; Londonderry.
68 Carmeran, Anne; Londonderry.
68 Carmeran, Elizabeth; Londonderry.
68 Carmeran, William; Londonderry.
4 Carmichael, Daniel; New York.
26 Carney, Anne; Wexford.
26 Carney, Eliza; Wexford.
48 Carney, John.
44 Carney, John.
26 Carney, John; Wexford.
26 Carney, Mary; Wexford.
26 Carney, Michael; Wexford.
26 Carney, Moses; Wexford.
26 Carney, Patrick; Wexford.
26 Carney, Philip; Wexford.
41 Carr, Elizabeth.
72 Carr, Isaac; Waterford.
53 Carr, John.
20 Carr, Nathaniel; Ballybuny.
61 Carr, Robert.
48 Carrigan, Andrew.
44 Carrigan, Patk.
55 Carroll, Mary.
2 Carroll, Rev. Michael; City of Kilkenny.
55 Carroll, Patrick.
65 Carroll, William; Co. Antrim.
55 Carroll, Terence.
42 Carslile, Hugh; Co. Down.
49 Carson, George.
23 Carson, James; Belfast.
13 Carter, Robert.
50 Caruthers. Archibald.
50 Caruthers, Jane.
50 Caruthers, John.
50 Caruthers, M.
72 Caselly, Patrick; Armagh.
18 Casey, Mr.; Dublin.
57 Casher, Anne; Wexford.
57 Casher, Bartholomew; Wexford.
57 Casher, M.; Wexford.
57 Casher, Margaret; Wexford.
28 Cassady, Anthony; Ballyshannon, Co. Donegal.
3 Cassady, James.
67 Cassell, Patrick; Armagh.
70 Castello, John.
54 Castello, Michael; Magheraw.
54 Castello, Thomas; Magheraw.
66 Castigan, Thomas; Meath.
53 Castlewood, Hugh.
48 Cathcart, Alexander.
48 Cathcart, Catherine.
39 Catherwood, Thomas.
31 Caughey, Mary; Dramore, Co. Down.
68 Causland, William; Tyrone.
1 Cavanagh, John; Dublin.
36 Cay, James.

36 Cay, Michael.
67 Chambers, Agnes; Danaghdee.
50 Chambers, Eliza.
67 Chambers, Eliza; Danaghdee.
50 Chambers, Charles.
67 Chambers, James; Danaghdee.
67 Chambers, Margaret; Danaghdee.
67 Chambers, Margaret; Danaghdee.
67 Chambers, Mary; Danaghdee.
67 Chambers, Mathew; Danaghdee.
67 Chambers, Robert; Danaghdee.
67 Chambers, Robert; Danaghdee.
67 Chambers, Sarah; Danaghdee.
20 Chambers, Thomas II; Aughterm.
67 Chambers, William; Danaghdee.
61 Chapman, William.
42 Charters, Arthur; Co. Down.
7 Charters, John; Antrim.
50 Chestnut, C.
50 Chestnut, M.
50 Chestnut, S.
16 Chestnut, William; Coleraine.
20 Christa, Adam; Ballymena.
55 Christian, John.
61 Christy, David.
32 Christy, Elizabeth.
32 Christy, Jane.
32 Christy, John.
32 Christy, Adam.
32 Christy, Robert.
43 Clancey, James; Co. Wexford.
55 Clancey, John.
72 Clancy, Robert; Athlone.
2 Clark, Charles; King's Court, Co. Cavan.
42 Clark, Hugh; Co. Down.
61 Clark, Jane.
19 Clark, John.
4 Clark, John; Co. Armagh.
33 Clark, John; Aughnamulin, Ballybay.
61 Clark, Margaret.
61 Clark, Matthew.
68 Clark, Neil; Tyrone.
5 Clark, Richard & wife; Waterford.
47 Clark, William.
16 Clark, William; Stonyford.
21 Clarke, James.
64 Claughey, —; Co. Armagh.
64 Claughey, James; Co. Armagh.
64 Claughey, John; Co. Armagh.
64 Claughey, Mary; Co. Armagh.
64 Claughey, Sarah; Co. Armagh.
72 Clear, Mary; Kilkenny.
57 Cleary, Andrew; Wexford.
6 Clebborn, Samuel.
24 Clegg, Joseph.
41 Clements, James.
41 Clements, Margaret.
2 Clinch, James; Bailiborough.
54 Clinton, Bartholomew; Grange.
50 Cloane, W.
25 Clock, Mathw. & wife.
44 Coach, Isabella.
44 Coach, John.
44 Coach, William.
8 Cochran, Agnes; Grange.
8 Cochran, Isaac; Grange.
8 Cochran, Jane; Grange.
8 Cochran, Mary Ann; Grange.
8 Cochran, Richard; Grange.
68 Cochran, Robert; Londonderry.
41 Cochran, Samuel.
15 Codd, Edward; Wexford.
15 Codd, James; Wexford.
36 Coghlan, Bridget.
36 Coghlan, Catherine.

36 Coghlan, Catherine.
36 Coghlan, Eliza.
36 Coghlan, Mary.
36 Coghlan, Patrick.
2 Cogly, Martin; Wexford.
27 Cole, John.
14 Coleman, Robert, wife & child.
48 Colhoun, John.
67 Coling, Peter; Morrill.
48 Coll, Dennis.
13 Collins, William.
13 Collins, William.
36 Concannon, John.
36 Concannon, William.
48 Coneghan, Patrick.
47 Conerry, John.
36 Connell, Patrick.
55 Connellin, James.
70 Connelly, Mary.
5 Connelly, Peter; Waterford.
14 Conner, Edward.
6 Conner, Jeremiah.
14 Conner, John.
3 Connolan, Thomas.
19 Connoly, Right Rev. Dr.
62 Connolly, Henry & wife.
48 Connor, John.
48 Connor, Hugh.
24 Connor, John.
43 Connor, Joseph; Wexford.
24 Connor, Michl.
24 Connor, Philip.
48 Connor, Richard.
15 Conolan, Charles; Ballybay.
15 Conolan, James; Ballybay.
44 Conolly, James.
55 Conolly, John.
55 Conolly, M.
54 Conolly, Thomas; Carrick on Shannon.
54 Conolly, Thomas; Darby.
55 Conolly, William.
50 Conolly, William J.
72 Conry, Catherine; Kilkenny.
59 Conry, James; Waterford.
72 Conry, Judith; Kilkenny.
72 Conry, Mary; Kilkenny.
72 Conry, Michael; Kilkenny.
3 Conway, Hugh.
68 Cook, Jos.; Tyrone.
55 Cook, Thomas.
63 Cook, Thomas; Co. Carlow.
68 Cooke, David; Londonderry.
68 Cooke, Hugh; Londonderry.
43 Corish, James; Wexford.
56 Corkoran, Michael.
61 Cornwell, John.
8 Corry, Hugh; Cookstown.
49 Corry, James.
43 Cosgrave, James; Wexford.
62 Cosgrove, Thomas.
3 Costello, Thomas.
72 Costigan, James; Dublin.
62 Cotter, Arthur.
5 Coughlan, James; Waterford.
49 Coulta, James.
68 Coulter, John; Tyrone.
67 Covenagh, Robert; Donegal.
13 Cowan, Charles.
29 Coyle, Francis; Co. Fermanagh.
68 Craig, Andrew, Tyrone.
49 Craig, Samuel.
4 Crany, John; Co. Down.
36 Craven, John.
37 Crawford, Anne & 3 children.
48 Crawford, David.
61 Crawford, English.
50 Crawford, J.

46 Crawford, James; Donegal.
68 Crawford, James; Londonderry.
49 Crawford, John.
68 Crawford, John; Londonderry.
50 Crawford, M.
46 Crawford, Mary; Donegal.
13 Crawford, William.
8 Crawford, William; Belfast.
23 Crawley, Lewis; Dublin.
23 Crawley, Michael; Dublin.
39 Crawlon, Patrick.
50 Creighton, James.
13 Crocket, James
13 Crocket, John.
33 Crooks, James; Moneymore, Co. Derry.
68 Crosby, Robert; Tyrone.
62 Crosby, Thomas.
6 Cross, Margaret.
3 Crossan, Michael.
65 Crossen, Francis; Philadelphia.
37 Crumley, Eleanor & sister.
54 Cryan, Bridget; Aughnasare, Co. Roscommon.
54 Cryan, Catharine; Aughnasare, Co. Roscommon.
54 Cryan, James; Aughnasare, Co. Roscommon.
54 Cryan, Martin, Aughnasare, Co. Roscommon
54 Cryan, Mary; Aughnasare, Co. Roscommon.
54 Cryan, Mary; Aughnasare, Co. Roscommon.
54 Cryan, Michael; Aughnasare, Co. Roscommon.
54 Cryan, Patrick; Aughnasare, Co. Roscommon.
54 Cryan, Timothy; Aughnasare, Co. Roscommon.
70 Cullen, Allen.
7 Cullen, Mary; Mays.
4 Cumming, Hans; Co. Down.
4 Cumming, Tho.; Co. Down.
24 Cummins, Catherine.
36 Cummins, Thomas.
44 Cunnay, Thomas.
20 Cunningham, Alexander; Aughnacloy.
44 Cunningham, James.
14 Cunningham, John.
62 Curran, Peter.
48 Currant, Patrick.
54 Curred, Bartholomew; Grange.
54 Curred, Bryan; Grange.
54 Curred, Dominick; Grange.
62 Currell, Elizah.
62 Currell, Susannah.
41 Curry, Alexander.
70 Curry, Michael.
41 Curry, William.
66 Cusack, Patrick; Coothill.

D

68 Daily, Henry; Tyrone.
47 Dale, Daniel.
4 Dale, George; Co. Antrim.
47 Dale, John.
47 Dale, Samuel.
47 Dale, William.
16 Dallas, Alexander; Coleraine.
48 Dally, Edward.
3 Dalton, Henry.
5 Daly, Anthony; Waterford.
66 Daly, Bryan; Kilkenny.
66 Daly, Ellen and 3 children; Kilkenny.
71 Daly, Ellen, Parish of Kildare, Kings County.

71 Daly, Martin; Parish of Kildare, Kings County.
71 Daly, Michael; Parish of Kildare, Kings County.
68 Daly, P.; Tyrone.
71 Daly, William; Ballina, Co. Mayo.
1 Daly, Wm. George; Cavan.
19 Danaho, Patrick.
67 Danford, James; Caldatt.
67 Danford, Ralph; Letterkenny.
36 Daniel, James.
71 Dannan, John; Athlone, Co. Westmeath.
12 Darcey, Thos.; Goery.
66 Daren, Anne; Meath.
66 Davenport, Catherine; Dublin.
37 Davenport, James.
71 Davey, Cornelius; Curreigh, Co. Galway.
61 Davidson, John.
8 Davidson, William; Ballybanden.
68 Davies, John; Tyrone.
49 Davis, Henry.
39 Davis, Mary.
21 Davis, Owen.
28 Davison, Christ.; Stramore, Co. Down.
28 Davison, John; Stramore, Co. Down.
28 Davison, Sarah; Gilford, Co. Down.
28 Dawson, Hugh; Carnmoney, Co. Antrim.
52 Dawson, Robert.
28 Dawson, Sarah; Carnmoney, Co. Antrim.
7 Dawson, Washington; Belfast.
2 Deale, Francis; Granard.
48 Deary, James.
28 Deavlin, Danl., Derry.
28 Deavlin, Neil; Derry.
54 Deighan, Joseph; Dublin.
2 Delahunt, Thomas; Drogheda.
59 Delany, Nicholas, Kilkenny.
66 Dempsey, Catherine; Dublin.
7 Dempsey, John; Aghadowy.
63 Dempsey, John; Portarlington.
27 Dennisson, Richard.
48 Derlin, Anne.
2 Deroy, Edward; Dublin.
2 Deroy, James; Dublin.
67 Deulin, Wm.; Londonderry.
57 Devereaux, James; Wexford.
53 Devlin, John.
24 Devlin, Michl.
36 Dew, Thomas.
8 Deymour, William; Drumbo.
17 Deyr, John; Ireland.
50 Diamere, J.
62 Diamond, John.
53 Dickey, Samuel.
8 Dickson, David; Co. Derry.
62 Dickson, Eliza.
62 Dickson, Hugh.
62 Dickson, Jane.
53 Dickson, John.
62 Dickson, Mary Ann.
62 Dickson, Sally.
62 Dickson, Samuel.
71 Dillan, David; Ballywaslee, Co. Galway.
24 Dillon, Ellen.
24 Dillon, James.
15 Dillon, John; Dublin.
38 Dillon, Patrick; Balbrigan.
24 Dillon, Richard.
70 Discord, J.
46 Diver, Edward; Donegal.
48 Diver, George.
48 Diver, Mary.

41 Diver, Patrick.
48 Diver, Sidney.
48 Diver, Susan.
48 Diver, William.
43 Dixon, Catherine; Co. Wexford.
37 Dixon, John.
13 Doak, Margaret.
13 Doak, Michael.
7 Dobson, Fanny; Moy.
7 Dobson, James; Moy.
7 Dobson, John; Moy.
7 Dobson, Mary; Moy.
7 Dobson, Susan; Moy.
7 Dobson, William; Moy.
52 Doffin, Wm.
41 Dogherty, Anne.
48 Dogherty, Michael.
48 Doherty, Anne.
61 Doherty, Anthony.
41 Doherty, Bryan.
8 Doherty, Catherine; Belfast.
8 Doherty, Catherine; Belfast.
54 Doherty, Charles; Coothall, Co. Roscommon.
48 Doherty, David.
48 Doherty, Daniel.
8 Doherty, Daniel; Belfast.
48 Doherty, Hugh.
48 Doherty, John.
68 Doherty, Maria; Londonderry.
8 Doherty, Mary; Belfast.
48 Doherty, Michael.
48 Doherty, Philip.
48 Doherty, William.
51 Doly, Arthur.
51 Doly, Altha.
51 Doly, Jane.
51 Doly, Henrietta.
51 Doly, Henrietta.
51 Doly, Maria.
48 Donaghe, Henry.
13 Donaghy, Anne.
13 Donaghy, Anne.
13 Donaghy, John.
49 Donnell, Daniel.
48 Donnell, James.
48 Donnelly, James.
28 Donnelly, John; Stuartstown, Co. Tyrone.
48 Donnelly, Patrick.
48 Donnelly, Robert.
63 Donoher, Simon; Co. Kildare.
1 Donohoo, James, Co. Meath.
68 Doogan, John; Tyrone.
5 Dooling, Michael; Waterford.
56 Dooney, John.
22 Doran, Paul; Wexford.
20 Dougherty, Bridget; Derry.
20 Dougherty, James; Derry.
46 Dougherty, John; Donegal.
37 Dougherty, William.
7 Douglass, Andrew; Belfast.
20 Douglass, James, Derry.
20 Dowe, Thomas; Aughterm.
72 Dowling, Michael; Kilkenny.
15 Downey, Michael; Dublin.
22 Doyle, Eliza and child; Dublin.
35 Doyle, John; Co. Wexford.
35 Doyle, Margaret; Co. Wexford.
35 Doyle, Martin; Strabane.
22 Doyle, Moses; Wexford.
42 Doyle, Patrick; Co. Down.
22 Doyle, Patrick; Wexford.
15 Doyne, Charles; Dublin.
62 Drain, John.
62 Drain, Richard.
16 Dripps, James; Maghera.

12 Dudley, Margaret; Roscrea.
4 Duff, Eliza; Co. Tyrone.
43 Duff, Jane; Dublin.
43 Duff, John; Dublin.
43 Duff, Margaret; Dublin.
8 Duff, Samuel; Co. Tyrone.
43 Duff, Thomas; Dublin.
37 Duffin, Anne.
71 Duffy, Charles; Coldaragh.
48 Duffy, Fanny.
71 Duffy, John; Parish of Kildare, Kings County.
72 Duffy, Mary and child; Carrickmacross.
48 Duffy, Patrick
48 Duffy, Patrick.
35 Duffy, Peter; Dundalk.
24 Duigan, Anne.
24 Duigan, Bridget.
24 Duigan, Eliza.
24 Duigan, Wm.
27 Duncan, Richard.
8 Duncan, William; Magherafelt.
27 Duneen, Daniel.
63 Duney, Robert; Co. Carlow.
57 Dunn, Elizabeth; Kings County.
57 Dunn, Mary; Kings County.
57 Dunn, Mathew; Kings County.
57 Dunn, Peter; Kings County.
57 Dunn, William; Kings County.
72 Dwyer, John; Kilkenny.
21 Dycle, John.
21 Dycle, Robert.

E

70 Eagan, Patrick.
68 Eager, Robert; Tyrone.
70 Earrie, Edward.
55 Edwards, Richard; Drimshambo.
5 Egan, Thomas; Waterford.
41 Elder, James.
48 Elder, John.
9 Elliot, J.; Dublin.
31 Elliot, Rev. Robert.
59 Ellis, Bartholomew; Dublin.
59 Ellis, Joseph; Dublin.
4 Ellison, John; Belfast.
46 Elliston, Robert; Donegal.
63 Elms, James; Co. Carlow.
60 Ennis, George; Enniscorthy.
6 Ennis, Mark.
28 Erwin, James; Ballybay, Co. Monaghan.
19 Erwin, John.
19 Erwin, Mary.
19 Erwin, Mary.
25 Evans, Wm.
7 Everitt, William; Belfast.
56 Evins, Samuel.
10 Ewing, Alexander D.; Londonderry.

F

15 Fagan, Michael; Dublin.
36 Fahey, Garrit.
36 Fahey, Mary.
36 Fahey, Tim. T.
71 Fahy, Andrew; Leitrim.
23 Fair, Alexander; Dublin.
3 Faley, Thomas.
66 Faley, William; Queens County.
70 Falin, Mary.
70 Fallan, William.
56 Farley, Owen.
28 Farmer, John; Belfast.
19 Farms, Ellen.
19 Farms, Mary.

19 Farms, Robert.
71 Farrel, Anne; Athlone, Co. Westmeath.
66 Farrel, Edward; Dublin.
35 Farrell,—; Philadelphia.
2 Farrell, Miss; Drogheda.
23 Farrell, Ellen; Tyrone.
56 Farrell, Peter.
9 Farrell, Richard; Co. Meath.
72 Farrell, William James; Dublin.
44 Faulkender, Patk.
19 Fax, Peter.
28 Fay, James; Castleblaney, Co. Monaghan.
1 Fay, Luke; Navan.
49 Fay, Patrick.
42 Fearis, Catherine; Co. Down.
42 Fearis, John; Co. Down.
42 Fearis, John; Co. Down.
42 Fearis, Margaret; Co. Down.
42 Fearis, Margaret; Co. Down.
42 Fearis, Mary; Co. Down.
46 Fee, Hugh; Donegal.
70 Feeney, Martin.
54 Feeny, Michael; Magheraw.
2 Fegan, Nich. & wife; Castle Pollard.
24 Fegan, Richd.
58 Fennely, Patrick; Kilkenny City.
25 Fenton, Geo.
46 Fergue, Eliza; Donegal.
46 Fergue, James; Donegal.
3 Ferguson, Charles.
54 Ferguson, Eleanor; Drumcliff.
62 Ferguson, Eliza.
54 Ferguson, Edward; Drumcliff.
67 Ferguson, James; Londonderry.
4 Ferguson, John; Co. Down.
54 Ferguson, John; Drumcliff.
62 Ferguson, Mary Ann.
13 Ferguson, Mathew.
62 Ferguson, Sally.
62 Ferguson, Susannah.
62 Ferguson, William & wife.
40 Ferris, David; Newry.
62 Ferris, James.
13 Fevry, Hugh.
15 Field, John; Dublin.
61 Fife, John.
61 Fife, Mary.
6 Finegan, Thomas.
4 Fingusin, Michael; Co. Tyrone.
33 Finigan, Hugh.
59 Finigan, James; Dublin.
40 Finigan, Matthew; Drogheda.
54 Finlan, Bridget; Mount Temple.
54 Finlan, James; Mount Temple.
54 Finlan, John; Mount Temple.
54 Finlan, Mary; Mount Temple.
54 Finlan, Mary; Mount Temple.
54 Finlan, Owen; Mount Temple.
54 Finlan, Patrick; Mount Temple.
48 Finlay, Charles.
38 Finn, James; Dublin.
41 Fisher, Hugh.
53 Fisher, James, wife & 5 children.
41 Fisher, Margaret.
41 Fisher, Michael.
19 Fitzgerald, John.
19 Fitzgerald, Mary.
16 Fitzgerald, Matthew; Larne.
14 Fitzgerald, Thomas.
26 Fitzgerald, Thomas; Queens County.
25 Fitzpatrick, Bernd.
56 Fitzpatrick, Daniel.
26 Fitzpatrick, Dennis; Queens County.
26 Fitzpatrick, Edmund; Kilkenny.
26 Fitzpatrick, James; Dublin.
26 Fitzpatrick, Mary Ann; Queens Co.

26 Fitzpatrick, Sally; Queens County.
26 Fitzpatrick, Terence; Cavan.
26 Fitzpatrick, Thomas; Queens County.
38 Flaherty, Margaret; Dublin.
13 Flaherty, Patrick.
54 Flanagan, Dominick; Mullaghmore.
24 Flanagan, Patrick.
39 Flanagan, Patrick.
71 Flanagan, Samuel; Parish of Kildare, Kings County.
56 Flemming, William.
51 Flinn, James.
30 Flinn, William; Banbridge.
5 Flood, Daniel; Waterford.
4 Flood, Samuel; Derry.
29 Flurn, Pack; Dublin.
59 Flushing, Eleanor; Carlow.
59 Flushing, George; Carlow.
59 Flushing, John; Carlow.
27 Flyn, James.
55 Flynn, Hugh; Ballifarnan.
38 Flynn, John; Balbrigan.
38 Flynn, John, Jun.; Balbrigan.
54 Flynn, Joseph; Drumahare.
38 Flynn, Mary; Balbrigan.
55 Foley, Anne; Sligo.
54 Foley, William; Mount Temple.
70 Folin, Bryan.
68 Forbes, Fanny; Tyrone.
68 Forbes, Jane; Tyrone.
68 Forbes, John; Tyrone.
68 Forbes, William, Junr.; Tyrone.
68 Forbes, William, Senr.; Tyrone.
27 Forest, John.
8 Forsyth, George; Magherafelt.
13 Forsyth, James.
35 Fortune, Patrick; Co. Wexford.
8 Foster, —; Belfast.
9 Foster, John; Co. Tyrone.
13 Frame, John.
23 Francis, Miss Day; Liverpool.
23 Francis, Joseph Day; Bath, England.
23 Francis, Redmond Day; Liverpool.
15 Frayne, James; Dublin.
15 Frayne, William; Dublin.
7 Frazer, Eliza; Belfast.
7 Frazer, Jane; Belfast.
7 Frazer, John; Belfast.
7 Frazer, Joseph; Belfast.
7 Frazer, Margaret; Belfast.
7 Frazer, Sarah; Belfast.
54 Freal, Honor; Mount Temple.
54 Freal, Owen; Mount Temple.
70 Froheley, Daniel.
70 Fuman, Michael.
13 Funston, Anne.
13 Funston, Francis.
13 Funston, John.
13 Funston, Joseph.
13 Funston, Robert.
43 Furlong, John; Wexford.
57 Furlong, Mathew; Wexford.
41 Fulton, —.
41 Fulton, Catherine.
41 Fulton, Kearns.

G

6 Gafney, James.
67 Galangher, James; Letterkenny.
19 Galbraith, Anne.
13 Galbraith, Charles.
19 Galbraith, Eliza.
13 Galbraith, William.
19 Galbraith, William.
19 Galbreath, James.
19 Galbreath, Rachael.

55 Galey, Anne; Sligo.
55 Galey, Eliza; Sligo.
46 Galey, William; Tyrone
46 Galey, Wister; Tyrone.
49 Gallager, Bridget.
49 Gallager, Peter.
45 Gallagher, Betsey.
45 Gallagher, Hugh.
13 Gallagher, Hugh.
13 Gallagher, John.
45 Gallagher, Michael.
20 Gallagher, Patrick; Bellybeggs.
54 Gallagher, Patrick; Teeling, Co. Donegal.
20 Gallagher, Roger; Derry.
34 Gallagher, Thomas; Co. Sligo.
20 Gallagher, William; Strabane.
41 Gamble, James.
3 Gamel, Andrew.
29 Ganly, John; Co. Antrim.
29 Ganly, Thomas; Co. Antrim.
71 Ganner, Dennis; Asker, Co. Galway.
29 Gannan, Hugh; Dublin.
71 Gannon, William; Parish of Kildare, Kings County.
68 Ganway, Bernard; Tyrone.
7 Gardner, Arthur; Belfast.
7 Gardner, Arthur, jun.; Belfast.
7 Gardner, Debarah; Belfast.
7 Gardner, Eleanor; Belfast.
7 Gardner, Elizabeth; Belfast.
7 Gardner, Elizabeth; Belfast.
53 Gardner, James.
29 Garelan, William; Co. Cavan.
39 Garney, Michel.
7 Garrett, Hugh; Saintfield.
48 Garven, William.
13 Gault, G.
49 Gault, George.
20 Gault, Robert; Coleraine.
20 Gault, Thompson; Coleraine.
52 Gausley, Jno.
27 Geary, Patrick.
63 Geohegan, Christopher; Co. Dublin.
14 Geoghegan, Henry.
14 Geoghegan, Murtoch.
39 George, John.
54 Gereghy, Paul; Mount Temple.
67 German, Patrick; Morrill.
50 Gibbons, H.
50 Gibbons, J.
50 Gibbons, M.
69 Gibbs, John; Co. Cavan.
69 Gibbs, John; Sligo.
69 Gibbs, Mary; Sligo.
69 Gibbs, Ruth; Sligo.
46 Gibson, Ann; Tyrone.
61 Gibson, Hugh.
62 Gibson, James.
61 Gibson, James.
32 Gibson, John.
61 Gibson, Margaret.
21 Gibson, Robert.
45 Gilfillin, John.
3 Gillan, Darby.
3 Gillan, Sally.
4 Gillen, Henry; Co. Antrim.
70 Gillen, John.
54 Gillen, Patrick; Magheraw.
50 Gillespie, Eliza.
13 Gillespie, Isabella.
50 Gillespie, James.
50 Gillespie, Mary.
50 Gillespie, Mary Anne.
13 Gillilan, William.
19 Gillin, Francis.
19 Gillin, James.

19 Gillin, Margaret.
70 Gillown, Anne.
70 Gillown, Owen.
61 Gilmore, Christopher.
65 Gilmore, James; Co. Tyrone.
19 Gilmore, John.
61 Gilmore, John.
61 Gilmore, John.
40 Gilmore, Margaret; Portadown, Co. Armagh.
61 Gilmore, Mary.
61 Gilmore, Matthew.
40 Gilmore, William; Portadown, Co. Armagh.
40 Gilmore, William jun.; Portadown, Co. Armagh.
16 Gilmour, Felix; Randlestown.
48 Gilmour, Joseph.
16 Gilmour, Michael; Randlestown.
59 Gilson, John; Carlow.
53 Gitty, James.
53 Gitty, John.
17 Given, John; Ireland.
41 Given, Joseph.
61 Given, Samuel.
52 Glass, Robert.
41 Glassey, Matthew.
41 Glassey, Robert.
72 Glynn, Joseph; Co. Tipperary.
5 Godfrey, Thomas; Waterford.
5 Godkin, Henry; Waterford.
54 Golrich, Martin; Sligo.
3 Golrick, Terence.
59 Gonry, Eleanor; Waterford.
13 Goodman, Catherine.
13 Goodman, Richard.
23 Gordon, Elizabeth; Dumfries, Scotland.
23 Gordon, John; Dumfries, Scotland.
23 Gordon, John; Dumfries, Scotland.
72 Gordon, Thomas; Co. Cavan.
40 Gordon, William; Kilkeel, Co. Down.
54 Gore, Luke.
67 Gorman, Hugh; Morrill.
68 Gorman, Hugh; Tyrone.
67 Gorman, Mary; Morrill.
26 Gorman, Rev. Michael; Kilkenny.
61 Gorman, William.
68 Gormley, Bernard; Tyrone.
54 Gormley, Martin; Boyle.
69 Gorvorn, Michael; Sligo.
54 Goveran, Peter.
5 Gowan, Henry; Waterford.
37 Gowan, James.
9 Gowran, John; Dublin.
5 Grace, Francis; Waterford.
42 Gracey, William; Co. Down.
24 Grady, Wm.
31 Graham, Alexander & wife.
28 Graham, James; Carnmoney, Co. Antrim.
22 Graham, James; Westmeath.
21 Graham, John.
45 Graham, Martin.
71 Graham, Mary; Ballyfair, Co. Kildare.
13 Graham, Patrick.
71 Graham, Thomas; Ballyfair, Co. Kildare.
50 Granthorn, Henry I.
46 Gray, Ann; Strabane.
21 Gray, Henry.
49 Gray, Samuel.
8 Gray, William; Edinburg.
42 Green, Henry; Co. Down.
45 Green, James.
68 Green, James chls.; Donegal.
28 Greene, Hugh; Belfast.

66 Greenham, Mary; Meath.
66 Gregory, Bridget & 2 children; Cavan.
32 Grey, Isaac.
20 Grier, Alexander; Derry.
45 Griffiths, Henry.
48 Griswell, John.
48 Griswell, Mary.
48 Griswell, Robert.
48 Griswell, William.
51 Guirson, Robert.
70 Gunigle, James.
56 Gunn, Patrick.
62 Gurroll, Charles.
48 Guthrey, John.

H

35 Haaff, James; Co. Westmeath.
48 Hagan, Edward.
60 Hagan, James; Enniscorthy.
8 Hagan, John; Co. Tyrone.
52 Hair, John.
21 Hale, Robert.
49 Hall, William.
59 Halle, Thomas; Wexford.
57 Halpen, James; Kilkenny.
30 Halpin, Bernard; Drogheda.
52 Hamilton, Eliza.
50 Hamilton, W.
52 Hamilton, Wm.
46 Hamilton, William; Donegal.
33 Hammill, Patrick; Portadown.
49 Hammond, Hugh.
48 Hammond, Hugh.
59 Hanley, James; Tipperary.
59 Hanley, Mary; Tipperary.
22 Hanlon, John O.; Longford.
40 Hanna, Robert; Kilkeel, Co. Down.
70 Haran, Mary.
46 Harbison, Henry; Maherafelt.
7 Harbison, Samuel; Philadelphia.
20 Harcourt, Anne; Bushill.
20 Harcourt, Richard; Bushill.
56 Harding, John.
71 Hardman, Darby; Tyapien, Co. Galway.
54 Hargaden, Patrick; Grange.
68 Hargon, William; Londonderry.
48 Harkin, John.
66 Harkin, Laurence; Kildare.
66 Harkin, Mary & 3 children; Kildare.
54 Harkin, Patrick; Mount Temple.
33 Harper, Alexander; Shea Bridge, Co. Down.
32 Harper, William.
43 Harpur, William; Co. Wexford.
8 Harris, Mary; Richhill.
39 Harrison, James.
39 Harrison, Thomas.
55 Hart, Bridget.
69 Hart, Hugh; Grange.
69 Hart, Hugh; Sligo.
54 Hart, John.
9 Hart, John; Dublin.
55 Hart, Margaret.
55 Hart, Mark; Sligo.
68 Hartness, George; Tyrone.
48 Harvey, Anne.
48 Harvey, Catherine.
28 Harvey, Jacob; Limerick.
16 Haslett, Fortescue; Belfast.
68 Hassan, Alexander; Londonderry.
68 Hassan, John; Londonderry.
68 Hassen, Bryan; Londonderry.
43 Hatch, Thomas; Dublin.
41 Hawkins, Thomas.
56 Hawthorn, Bill.

43 Hawthorn, Ellen; Dublin.
56 Hawthorn, Esther.
56 Hawthorn, John.
56 Hawthorn, Thomas.
70 Hay, John.
69 Hay, John; Sligo.
49 Hay, Robert.
52 Hay, Robert.
28 Hay, William; Carrickfergus, Co. Antrim.
5 Hayden, Bridget; Waterford.
5 Hayden, Bridget, jun; Waterford.
35 Hayden, Patrick; Co. Wexford.
61 Hays, Thomas.
54 Healy, Bryan; Magheraw.
22 Healy, John; Dublin.
54 Healy, John; Grange.
70 Healy, Margaret.
54 Healy, Mary; Grange.
54 Healy, Michael; Grange.
54 Healy, Patrick; Grange.
56 Heany, Francis.
37 Heely, Mary.
13 Henderson, Anne.
13 Henderson, Catherine.
13 Henderson, Christopher.
50 Henderson, Eleanor.
13 Henderson, Francis.
47 Henderson, George.
13 Henderson, George.
50 Henderson, James.
17 Henderson, James; Ireland.
13 Henderson, Jane.
33 Henderson, John.
13 Henderson, John.
13 Henderson, John.
13 Henderson, Joseph.
70 Henderson, Robert.
13 Henderson, Robert.
47 Henderson, Thomas.
50 Henderson, William.
3 Henderson, William.
15 Henderson, William; Belfast.
13 Henderson, Williams.
27 Hendrick, Eliza.
27 Hendrick, John.
55 Henegan, James.
6 Henney, Peter.
63 Henry —, & daughter; Co. Meath.
70 Henry, Anne.
69 Henry, David; Sligo.
69 Henry, George; Sligo.
70 Henry, James W.
28 Henry, John; Cookstown, Co. Derry.
69 Henry, John; Sligo.
70 Henry, Samuel.
69 Henry, Samuel; Sligo.
69 Henry, Samuel; Sligo.
7 Henry, William; Belfast.
42 Herran, George; Co. Down.
4 Herrin, Thomas; Co. Down.
53 Hetherington, John.
53 Hetherington, Sarah & 5 children.
2 Hewett James; Killeschandra.
34 Hewit, David; Co. Antrim.
7 Hice, Eleanor; Drumgolen.
38 Hicks, Maurice; Kilkenny.
55 Higgins, John; Ballifarnan.
36 Higgins, Martin.
53 Hill, Adam.
48 Hill, Anne.
54 Hill, George; Scotland.
53 Hill, John.
40 Hill, John; Liverpool.
70 Hill, Martin.
48 Hill, Matilda.
39 Hill, Samuel.

48 Hill, Samuel.
7 Hill, Samuel; Ballycastle.
53 Hill, Thos.
25 Hobbart, Edward.
24 Hogan, Patk.
57 Holden, Edward; Wexford.
13 Holmes, George.
13 Holmes, James.
20 Holmes, John; Raphoe.
31 Holmes, Joseph; Dramore, Co. Down.
51 Hopkins, Mathew.
23 Hopkins, Samuel; Ballycastle.
20 Houston, James; Strabane.
66 Howell, John; Landaff.
15 Hoye, Patrick; Dublin.
45 Huey, Betty.
45 Huey, James.
63 Hugh, — .
59 Hughes, Charles; Dublin.
25 Hughes, Hugh.
50 Hughes, J.
45 Hughes, John.
61 Hughes, Patrick.
53 Hughes, Peter.
50 Hughes, S.
48 Hulton, Patrick.
51 Humphreys, Francis.
38 Hunt, Wilson A.; Dublin.
50 Hunter, Catherine.
50 Hunter, Charles.
68 Hunter, James; Londonderry.
68 Hunter, John; Londonderry.
68 Hunter, Mary; Londonderry.
68 Hunter, William; Londonderry.
49 Husson, James.
68 Hutton, James; Londonderry.
68 Hutton, Patrick; Londonderry.
71 Hynes, Edward; Melick, Co. Galway.

I

66 Ingraham, Thomas, wife & 9 children; Dublin.
51 Ingram, Farmer.
51 Ingram, Florena.
51 Ingram, Florena.
51 Ingram, John.
51 Ingram, Mary.
51 Ingram, Mary.
51 Ingram, Sally.
13 Irvine, Dary.
13 Irvine, Mr.
7 Irvine, James; Markethill.
13 Irvine, John.
20 Irvine, Robert; Ballindrate.
13 Irvine, William.
7 Irvine, William; Markethill.
66 Irwin, James; Coothill.
59 Ivers, Anne; Carlow.
59 Ivers, Catherine; Carlow.
59 Ivers, John; Carlow.
59 Ivers, R.; Carlow.
59 Ivers, Samuel G.; Carlow.
59 Ivers, William; Carlow.
1 Ivory, Chr., wife & child; Co. Limerick.

J

21 Jack, Robert.
68 Jackson, James; Londonderry.
64 James, Elizabeth; Castle Canfield.
32 James, Elizh.
32 James, Elizh.
32 James, Jane.
32 James, John.
32 James, John.
32 James, Joseph.

32 James, Mary.
32 James, Robert.
72 James, Thomas; New York.
32 James, William.
8 Jameson, Andrew; Grey Abbey.
50 Jameson, B.
4 Jameson, Hugh; Co. Antrim.
53 Jameson, J. & brother.
69 Janes, Roger; Sligo.
69 Janes, William; Sligo.
40 Jacques, John J.; Monmouth, New Jersey.
5 Jeffers, Anthony; Waterford.
57 Johnson, Catherine; Wexford.
5 Johnson, George; Waterford.
5 Johnson, Henry; Waterford.
72 Johnson, James; near Sheffield.
62 Johnson, Joseph.
5 Johnson, Martha, (a child); Waterford.
1 Johnson, Robert; Wicklow.
72 Johnson, Samuel; near Sheffield.
5 Johnson, Sarah; Waterford.
68 Johnson, William; Londonderry.
55 Johnston, —; Sligo.
39 Johnston, Anne.
68 Johnston, Archibald; Tyrone.
55 Johnston, Elizabeth; Sligo.
55 Johnston, Francis.
44 Johnston, Gera.
55 Johnston, Jane; Sligo.
44 Johnston, Mary.
44 Johnston, Oliver.
8 Johnston, Patrick; Ballymena.
15 Johnston, Robert; Cavan.
68 Johnston, Samuel; Tyrone.
44 Johnston, William.
13 Johnston, William.
55 Johnston, William; Sligo.
39 Jolly, Margaret.
39 Jolly, Robert.
69 Jones, Catherine; Sligo.
9 Jones, Henry; Dublin.
22 Jones, James; Dublin.
51 Jordain, Thomas.
57 Jordan, Dennis; Wexford.
26 Jordan, Richard; Dublin.
50 Jugant, James.

K

59 Kananak, Langn, Longford.
68 Kane, John; Londonderry.
56 Kane, Patrick.
66 Kane, Robert; Leitrim.
8 Keanen, Patrick; Richhill.
52 Kearney, Henry.
59 Kearney, James; Kildare.
59 Kearney, John; Kildare.
33 Kearney, Johnston; Armagh.
52 Kearney, Jno.
2 Kearns, Patrick; Dublin.
66 Keating, Anne & child; Kilkenny.
66 Keating, Edward; Kilkenny
60 Keating, Hugh; Kings County.
20 Keen, Samuel; Augher.
66 Keenan, Daniel; Upperwood.
66 Keenan, Ellen & child; Meath.
66 Keenan, Thomas; Meath.
69 Keeny, John; Sligo.
67 Keer, Alexander; Newtown Stewart.
24 Kehoe, Mary.
63 Kehoe, Michael; Co. Carlow.
43 Kehoe, Thomas; Co. Wexford.
56 Keirnan, James.
28 Keith, Rebecca; Belfast.
59 Kelly, Adam; Carlow.

54 Kelly, Charles; Carrick on Shannon.
15 Kelly, Anne & child; Dublin.
48 Kelly, Dudley.
59 Kelly, Edward; Carlow.
2 Kelly, Hugh; Banbridge.
2 Kelly, Hugh; Cavan.
59 Kelly, Hugh; Carlow.
35 Kelly, James; Co. Wexford.
24 Kelly, Jas.
59 Kelly, John; Carlow.
59 Kelly, John; Carlow.
54 Kelly, John; Drumahare.
2 Kelly, John; Dublin.
59 Kelly, Margaret; Carlow.
59 Kelly, Margaret; Carlow.
2 Kelly, Margaret; Cavan.
42 Kelly, Margaret; Co. Down.
29 Kelly, Margaret; Mount Melick.
66 Kelly, Mary; Carlow.
66 Kelly, Michael; Carlow.
54 Kelly, Michael; Drumahare.
63 Kelly, Michael; Co. Carlow.
9 Kelly, Miss; Dublin.
48 Kelly, Patrick.
59 Kelly, Richard; Carlow.
40 Kelly, Robert; Banbridge.
35 Kelly, Robert; Dublin.
57 Kelly, Thomas; Carlow.
59 Kelly, William; Carlow.
6 Kemple, John.
66 Kenedy, Bridget; Dublin.
66 Kenedy, John; Dublin.
51 Kennady, Val.
52 Kennedy, Alexander.
48 Kennedy, Alexander.
62 Kennedy, Andrew.
54 Kennedy, Anne; Grange
14 Kennedy, Edward.
54 Kennedy, John; Grange.
62 Kennedy, John & wife.
59 Kennedy, Joseph; Carlow.
19 Kennedy, Margaret.
26 Kennedy, Margaret; Dublin.
14 Kennedy, William.
62 Kennedy, William.
26 Kenny, Michael; Cavan.
13 Kernaghan, Robert.
14 Keown, James R.
27 Kerby, Mich.
13 Kerr, Alexander.
13 Kerr, Catherine.
3 Kerr, George.
45 Kerr, Henry.
13 Kerr, Isabella.
13 Kerr, James.
45 Kerr, John.
13 Kerr, John.
13 Kerr, Matilda.
45 Kerr, Nancy.
31 Kerr, Patrick; Monaghan.
45 Kerr, Robert.
8 Kerr, Robert; Ballymena.
45 Kerr, Thomas.
63 Kervan, Thos.; Phillipstown.
71 Kerrvan, Henry; St. Nicholas Galway.
46 Keys, Elizabeth; Donegal.
46 Keys, Samuel; Donegal.
39 Kidd, J.
23 Kield, Isaac; Dublin.
71 Kilfoyle, Peter; Parish of Kildare, Kings County.
6 Killen, Thomas.
70 Kilmartin, Charles.
54 Kilmartin, Hugh; Mount Temple.
54 Kilmartin, Hugh; Mullaghmore.
54 Kilmartin, John; Mount Temple.
54 Kilmartin, Mary; Mullaghmore.

54 Kilmartin, Patrick; Mullaghmore.
59 Kinanak, Matthew; Meath.
32 King, Thomas.
9 King, Thomas; Balbriggan.
61 Kingsland, John.
43 Kinshela, William; Co. Wexford.
20 Kirk, William; Buncrana.
48 Kirkpatrick, Alexander.
48 Kirkpatrick, And.
28 Kirkpatrick, Anne; Belfast.
48 Kirkpatrick, Crissey.
48 Kirkpatrick, Eliza.
46 Kirkpatrick, George; N. S. Stewart.
20 Kirkpatrick, George; Ringsend.
48 Kirkpatrick, Jane.
28 Kirkpatrick, John; Belfast.
28 Kirkpatrick, Margt.; Belfast.
28 Kirkpatrick, Mary; Belfast.
28 Kirkpatrick, Rob.; Belfast.
13 Knox, James.
13 Kyle, Elizabeth.
13 Kyle, Robert.
27 Kynn, John.

L

36 Laffey, James.
35 Lain, David; Dublin.
13 Laird, Andrew.
60 Lalor, Danl.; Queens County.
71 Lally, Michael; Buttersbridge, Co. Cavan.
15 Lambert, Anne; Birr.
72 Lambert, Margaret; Kilkenny.
71 Lambert, William; Lambert-Ledge, Co. Galway.
66 Lane, Mary Anne; Almerita.
15 Langley, Michael; Dublin.
43 Langton, Daniel; Kilkenny.
48 Laperty, Michael.
72 Laphen, Philip; Armagh.
60 Larkin, Patrick; Balbriggan.
9 Latham, Elias; Dublin.
60 Latham, Hannah; Queens County.
9 Latham, Henry; Dublin.
7 Latham, Hugh; Crumlin.
9 Latham, Martha; Dublin.
9 Latham, Nathaniel; Dublin.
9 Latham, Thomas & wife; Dublin.
9 Latham, William; Dublin.
48 Laughery, Isabella.
48 Laughlin, George.
52 Laughlin, Wm.
52 Laughran, Jas.
64 Laughton, Robert; Laughgall.
53 Law, John; Scotland.
34 Law, William; Co. Down.
63 Lawler, John, wife & child; Co. Kildare.
48 Lawn, Edward.
14 Lea, Robert.
60 Leahy, Henry; Dublin.
1 Lear, John; Dublin.
55 Leary, Matthew.
48 Leckey, Thomas.
56 Leddy, Michael.
25 Leddy, Mrs. & 2 children.
8 Lee, Alexander; Co. Cavan.
8 Lee, Anne; Co. Cavan.
8 Lee, Edward; Co. Cavan.
7 Lee, George; Moy.
8 Lee, Jane; Co. Cavan.
7 Lee, John; Moy.
8 Lee, Mary; Co. Cavan.
7 Lee, Sarah; Moy.
7 Lee, Simon; Moy.
7 Lee, Thomas; Moy.

68 Leech, A.; Tyrone.
67 Leech, Andrew; Balbriggan.
68 Leech, Malcolm; Tyrone.
67 Leech, Sarah; Balbrigan.
38 Left, Adam; Dublin.
20 Lester, Anne; Strabane.
20 Lester, John; Strabane.
68 Lighton, William; Londonderry.
71 Lilly, John; Buttersbridge, Co. Cavan.
41 Limerick, Alexander.
65 Linchey, James; Philadelphia.
55 Lingan, Bridget.
55 Lingan, John.
3 Lindsay, George.
55 Lindsay, Isabella; Sligo.
3 Lindsay, Richard.
3 Lindsay, Robert.
62 Lindsay, Susan.
4 Linn, Daniel; Co. Antrim.
72 Linnan, John; Dublin.
54 Little, Thomas; Carney.
13 Lockhart, John.
13 Lockhart, Margaret.
66 Lockwood, John; Leister.
13 Logan, Daniel.
30 Logan, John; Monaghan.
13 Logan, Thomas.
66 Long, Joseph; Cavan.
27 Long, William.
8 Longman, Robert; Rushmills.
20 Loony, Anne; Bushill.
26 Loughnan, Martin; Queens County.
48 Love, Alexander.
13 Love, Anne.
13 Love, Samuel.
8 Low, John; Co. Antrim.
13 Lowden, Robert.
64 Lowry, Samuel; Co. Tyrone.
64 Lowry, Thomas; Co. Tyrone.
59 Lucas, Eleanor; Dublin.
23 Luke, Samuel; Belfast.
2 Lynch, Bryan; King's Court, Co. Cavan.
48 Lynch, John.
18 Lynch, Mr.; Dublin.
19 Lynch, Patrick.
69 Lynch, Peter; Sligo.
48 Lynch, Susan.
19 Lynch, Thomas.
38 Lyndon, James; Dublin.
38 Lyndon, Mary.
35 Lynes, Peter; New York.
40 Lyons, William; Armagh.

M

61 MacAffer, Andrew.
61 MacAlister, Anthony; Antrim.
28 MacAlister, Daniel; Donegal; Co. Antrim.
53 MacAllignon, Rich.
48 MacAloo, Daniel.
69 MacAnalty, Patrick; Sligo.
37 MacArand, Patrick.
39 MacArdle, Anne.
39 MacArdle, John.
39 MacArdle, Mary Anne.
39 MacArdle, Owen.
39 MacArdle, Peter.
6 MacArnon, Mary.
7 MacAtier, James; Aghadowy.
26 MacAuley, James; Castleblaney.
44 MacBraty, Chs.
62 MacBride, Bernard.
4 MacBride, James; Co. Antrim.
48 MacBride, John.

46 MacBride, Patrick; Donegal.
42 MacBride, William; Co. Armagh.
2 MacCabe, John; Cavan.
31 MacCabe, Pat.; Ballybay, Co. Monaghan.
56 MacCabe, Terrence.
32 MacCall, Alex.
32 MacCall, Alice.
68 MacCallan, James; Londonderry.
42 MacCam, Felix; Co. Antrim.
8 MacCambridge, Alexander; Cushendun.
53 MacCambridge, Jas.
61 MacCanaghty, James.
68 MacCanaghy, David; Tyrone.
68 MacCanaghy, Mary; Tyrone.
34 MacCanbrey, Rich.; Co. Antrim.
22 MacCarfin, T.; Longford.
11 MacCarter, James; Ireland.
34 MacCanly, Robert; Co. Down.
39 MacCann, Bernard.
4 MacCann, Daniel; Derry.
45 MacCann, John.
39 MacCann, Owen.
14 MacCann, William.
31 MacCannell, Carry; Clare, Co. Armagh.
31 MacCannell, Samuel; Clare, Co. Armagh.
4 MacCarden, Edward; Co. Down.
61 MacCarker, Patrick.
66 MacCarthy, Bryan; Cavan.
62 MacCartney, Patrick.
4 MacCarty, Rose; Co. Armagh.
30 MacCaskey, Eliza; Aughnacloy.
30 MacCaskey, John; Aughnacloy.
14 MacCasle, Thomas.
26 MacCathen, Adam; Dublin.
46 MacCauley, Eliza; N. S. Stewart.
46 MacCauley, Elizabeth; N. S. Stewart.
37 MacCauley, Robert & brother.
30 MacCauly, Jane; Lurgan.
62 MacCauly, John.
30 MacCauly, John; Lurgan.
53 MacCausland, Andrew.
52 MacCawley, James.
48 MacClaskey, Dennis.
48 MacClaskey, Henry.
49 MacClaskey, Hugh.
50 MacClean, James.
50 MacClean, M.
4 MacCleary, Sam.; Co. Tyrone.
8 MacClelland, Mr.; Co. Down.
8 MacClelland, Mrs.; Co. Down.
8 MacClelland, James; Richhill.
8 MacClelland, Mary; Co. Down.
8 MacClelland, Samuel; Richhill.
8 MacClellon, William; Ballymena.
67 MacCloud, Anne; Londonderry.
67 MacCloud, Daniel; Londonderry.
67 MacCloud, James; Londonderry.
67 MacCloud, John; Londonderry.
67 MacCloud, Mary Anne; Londonderry.
67 MacCloud, Neile; Londonderry.
42 MacClushey, Matilda.
42 MacClushey, Martha.
41 MacCoal, Charles.
41 MacCoal, Patrick.
48 MacColgan, George.
46 MacColgan, John; Donegal.
13 MacColim, Daniel.
13 MacColim, Margaret.
39 MacColley, John.
13 MacCollison, David.
13 MacCollison, Thomas.
52 MacCollough, Wm.
68 MacComb, Daniel; Donegal.
48 MacComb, John.

61 MacConley, George.
66 MacConnell, James; Monaghan.
68 MacCool, James; Donegal.
3 MacCormack, B.
66 MacCormick, Esther; Leitrim.
53 MacCormick, James.
36 MacCormick, John.
52 MacCormick, Jno.
66 MacCormick, Patrick; Leitrim.
41 MacCoy, Alexander.
23 MacCracken, Alexander; Belfast.
23 MacCracken, Alexander, Jr.; Belfast.
23 MacCracken, Joseph; Belfast.
49 MacCrea, John.
49 MacCrea, John.
67 MacCrossin, John; Danaghdee.
1 MacCullagh, Michael; Dublin.
53 MacCulloch, James.
34 MacCullum, Joseph; Co. Antrim.
8 MacCurdy, James; Coleraine.
8 MacCurdy, Jane; Coleraine.
16 MacCurdy, John; Ballycastle.
16 MacCurdy, Neil; Ballycastle.
8 MacCurdy, William; Coleraine.
68 MacCusker, Terence; Tyrone.
41 MacDaid, John.
22 MacDaniel, Mrs. & child; Kildare.
22 MacDaniel, And'w; Kilkenny.
62 MacDaniel, John.
66 MacDaniel, Less; Kilkenny.
6 MacDaniel, Mary.
6 MacDaniel, Michael.
66 MacDaniel, Owen; Kilkenny.
22 MacDaniel, T.; Kildare.
22 MacDaniel, Tho.; Kilkenny.
51 MacDemiott, Peter.
66 MacDermot, John; Meath.
41 MacDermott, Charles.
47 MacDermott, Daniel.
63 MacDermott, John.
41 MacDermott, Mary.
63 MacDermott, Owen.
43 MacDermott, Owen; New York.
24 MacDermott, Patk.
41 MacDermott, Patrick.
41 MacDermott, Rose.
41 MacDermott, Susannah.
41 MacDermott, William.
41 MacDermott, William.
53 MacDill, John; Scotland.
69 MacDonagh, James; Sligo.
70 MacDonald, Thos.
66 MacDonel, James; Queens County.
63 MacDonnel, —; Co. Meath.
72 MacDonnell, Judith; Thurles.
72 MacDonnell, Margaret; Thurles.
72 MacDonnell, Michael; Thurles.
61 MacDonnell, Robert.
61 MacDonnell, Thomas.
3 MacDougal, John.
3 MacDougal, Mary.
67 MacDougal, Mary; Letterkenny.
67 MacDougall, John; Letterkenny.
50 MacDowel, C.
50 MacDowel, C.
50 MacDowel, John.
50 MacDowel, M.
50 MacDowel, W.
16 MacDowell, Alexander; Dromore.
42 MacDowell, John; Co. Down.
65 MacEvoy, Edward; Co. Tyrone.
39 MacEvoy, Owen.
48 MacFadden, Charles.
13 MacFadden, Samuel.
41 MacFarland, Robert.
46 MacFarlane, John; Maherafelt.
53 MacGaragher, J., wife & 5 children.

54 MacGaraghy, Bryan; Mount Temple.
44 MacGattiger, Daniel.
44 MacGavaran, John.
28 MacGeoch, Ellen; Ballybay, Co. Monaghan.
28 MacGeoch, Grace; Glymluse, Wigtonshire.
28 MacGeoch, Sam.; Newtown Stewart.
62 MacGibbon, Samuel.
28 MacGill, Robert; Cookstown, Co. Derry.
68 MacGinn, Rose; Tyrone.
48 MacGinnis, Daniel.
34 MacGinnis, Daniel; Co. Antrim.
48 MacGinnis, Ellen.
48 MacGinnis, Henry.
47 MacGinnis, John.
48 MacGinnis, Owen.
48 MacGinnis, Thomas.
16 MacGladery, Samuel; Stillwater.
55 MacGlam, John.
55 MacGlam, Patrick.
13 MacGlaughlin, Robert.
48 MacGloin, Edward.
55 MacGloin, Henry.
55 MacGloin, John.
54 MacGloin, Margaret; Tauly.
55 MacGloin, Mary & child.
13 MacGloughlin, Dennis.
13 MacGloughlin, Mary.
13 MacGloughlin, Patrick.
68 MacGlyn, Catherine; Tyrone.
48 MacGongle, Henry.
7 MacGouran, Samuel; Comber.
6 MacGovern, Charles.
61 MacGowan, Andrew.
48 MacGowan, Dennis.
68 MacGowan, Dennis; Tyrone.
13 MacGowan, James.
4 MacGowan, James; Co. Antrim.
54 MacGowan, John; Dunally.
61 MacGowan, Mary.
55 MacGowan, Patrick.
48 MacGowan, Patrick.
20 MacGowan, Bernard; Newtown Stewart.
69 MacGown, Andrew; Sligo.
50 MacGra, John.
48 MacGranahan, Thomas.
19 MacGrath, James.
37 MacGrath, William.
68 MacGreevy, Patrick; Tyrone.
61 MacGrery, James.
61 MacGrery, Margaret.
20 MacGrier, Robert; Armagh.
60 MacGrim, Bryan; Drogheda.
55 MacGuire, Bridget.
31 MacGuire, Ellen; Mullingar, Co. Westmeath.
55 MacGuire, Mary.
68 MacGum, Patrick; Tyrone.
68 MacGuragle, Robert; Londonderry.
62 MacGuskin, A.
48 MacHale, Thomas.
70 MacHugh, Andrew.
49 MacIlhames, John.
67 MacIlheny, Robert; Letterkenny.
8 MacIlrath, King; Co. Antrim.
23 MacIlroy, Charles; Down.
62 MacIlroy, Patrick.
23 MacIlroy, Mrs.; Down.
13 MacIntire, James.
13 MacIntire, Robert.
62 MacIntire, Robt.
13 MacIntire, Samuel.
67 MacIntosh, Jane; Danaghdee.
67 MacIntosh, William; Danaghdee.

4 MacKay, Alexander; Co. Antrim.
43 MacKay, Eliza; Co. Dublin.
14 MacKay, Francis.
43 MacKay, James; Co. Dublin.
50 MacKay, P.
50 MacKay, S.
43 MacKay, William; Co. Dublin.
39 MacKee, Robert.
4 MacKee, Robert & wife; Co. Antrim.
40 MacKee, William; Kilkeel, Co. Down.
23 MacKell, Thomas; New York.
50 MacKeene, Peter.
53 MacKeighan, —.
16 MacKennan, Bernart; Monaghan.
16 MacKennan, Patrick; Monaghan.
16 Mackeon, Isabella; Ballymena.
65 MacKeon, Robt.; Co. Tyrone.
16 MacKeon, Rose; Randlestown.
16 Mackeon, William; Ballymena.
68 MacKeown, Anne; Tyrone.
68 MacKeown, John, Junr.; Tyrone.
68 MacKeown, John Senr.; Tyrone.
68 MacKeown, Margaret; Tyrone.
68 MacKeown, Mary; Tyrone.
68 MacKeown, Mary; Tyrone.
68 MacKeown, Saml.; Tyrone.
68 MacKeown, Samuel; Tyrone.
68 MacKeown, Sarah; Tyrone.
68 MacKeown, William; Tyrone.
61 Mackerill, James.
61 Mackerill, Jane.
61 Mackerill, Thomas.
9 MacKernan, Edward; Co. Leitrim.
9 MacKernan, Patrick; Co. Leitrim.
25 Mackeson, James.
35 MacKevers, Peter; Co. Louth.
37 MacKey, Eleanor.
61 MacKill, Thos.
53 MacKinne, John.
33 MacKinstry, John.
54 MacKninon, Hannah; Mullaghmore.
20 MacLachling, John; Derry.
60 MacLain, John; Drogheda.
45 MacLaughlin, Cornelius.
48 MacLaughlin, Dennis.
67 MacLaughlin, Dennis.
72 MacLaughlin, Edward; Kilkenny.
61 MacLaughlin, Hugh.
39 MacLaughlin, James.
54 MacLaughlin, James; Drumahare.
71 MacLaughlin, James; Somerset, Co. Galway.
48 MacLaughlin, John.
71 MacLaughlin, John; Somerset, Co. Galway.
61 MacLaughlin, Margaret.
68 MacLaughlin, Mary; Londonderry.
41 MacLaughlin, Peter.
48 MacLaughlin, Philip.
48 MacLaughlin, Sarah.
3 MacLean, Bridget.
3 MacLean, Owen.
8 MacLean, Peter; Co. Derry.
25 MacLean, Thomas.
61 MacLorran, William.
19 MacMahon, Bridget.
61 MacMail, Hugh.
70 MacMarrow, Mary.
70 MacMarrow, Owen.
70 MacManus, Bernard.
40 MacManus, Bernard; Cavan.
2 MacManus, Michael; Killeshandra.
25 MacManus, Nathl., wife & 2 children.
56 MacManus, Patrick.
3 MacManus, Patrick.
41 MacMenamy, John.

41 MacMenamy, Peter.
67 MacMenomy, Elizabeth; Letterkenny.
67 MacMenomy, Elizabeth; Letterkenny.
48 MacNenomy, Hugh.
67 MacMenomy, Hugh; Letterkenny.
68 MacMenomy, John; Donegal.
67 MacMenomy, Robt., Letterkenny.
67 MacMenomy, Thomas; Letterkenny.
67 MacMenomy, William; Letterkenny.
13 MacMiller, Gideon.
4 MacMullen, Alexander; Co. Antrim.
28 MacMullen, Catherine; Lurgan, Co. Armagh.
61 MacMurray, Archibald.
28 MacMurray, David; Ballybay, Co. Monaghan.
28 MacMurray, Jess; Belfast.
68 MacNarna, Wm.; Tyrone.
22 MacNarney, John; Longford.
22 MacNarney, Michael; Longford.
8 MacNaughten, John; Monaghan.
68 MacNemee, Francis; Tyrone.
13 MacNeremon, William.
54 MacNulty, Wm.; Tauly.
68 MacPhilaney, Margaret; Tyrone.
70 MacPhiloron, Dennis.
61 MacQueen, Matthew.
62 MacQuig, William.
39 MacQuinn, Patrick.
16 MacQuoid, James; Clogher.
8 MacRalin, Roger; Ballymena.
41 MacRedden, James.
68 MacSerley, James; Tyrone.
13 MacShane, Daniel.
14 MacSheldon, James.
54 MacSherry, Patrick; Darby.
68 MacSwigon, Mary; Tyrone.
68 MacSwigon, Philip; Tyrone.
62 MacTahan, Henry & wife.
42 MacTea, Arthur; Co. Down.
62 MacTice, Andrew.
68 MacVaid, James; Tyrone.
52 MacVea, Jas.
68 MacVeigh, Henry; Tyrone.
16 MacVicker, Thos.; Larne.
48 MacVoy, Dominick.
9 Madden, James; Kilkenny.
22 Madden, James; Slane.
19 Madigan, Ally.
19 Madigan, Anne.
19 Madigan, Edward.
19 Madigan, James.
19 Madigan, Judy.
19 Madigan, Mary.
19 Madigan, Peggy.
19 Madigan, Walter.
19 Madigan, Walter.
19 Madigan, William.
23 Magee, Bernard; Dublin.
32 Magee, Bernd.
62 Magee, James.
62 Magee, John.
62 Magee, John.
35 Magee, John; Kilkenny.
35 Magee, Patrick; Kilkenny.
62 Magee, William.
53 Magher, —.
23 Magill, Daniel; Dublin.
20 Magill, John; Killetter.
12 Maguire, Henry; Dublin.
50 Mahany, John.
50 Mahany, Mary.
50 Mahany, Mary.
50 Mahany, Mary J.
38 Mahon, Catherine; Kilkenny.
56 Mahon, Charles.
38 Mahon, Joseph; Kilkenny.

27 Mahony, F.
5 Mahony, Jas.; Wexford, a citizen of U. S.
15 Maiben, Mrs. Jane & child; Dublin.
15 Maiben, Richard; New York.
34 Malcomson, Adam; Co. Down.
2 Malone, Francis; Killeshandra.
6 Malone, Henry.
45 Malsey, Mary.
26 Maly, John; Dublin.
42 Manning, William; Co. Antrim.
69 Mara, James; Lurgonboy.
14 March, Charles.
24 Marfelt, John.
28 Markey, James; Ballybay, Co. Monaghan.
8 Marshall, Isabella; Co. Antrim.
8 Marshall, John; Co. Antrim.
8 Marshall, Margaret; Co. Antrim.
8 Marshall, Mary; Co. Antrim.
8 Marshall, Samuel; Co. Antrim.
62 Marshall, William.
65 Martin, Andrew; Co. Antrim.
61 Martin, George.
22 Martin, Hugh; Kildare.
44 Martin, James.
30 Martin, James; Markethill.
46 Martin, James; N. S. Stewart.
62 Martin, John.
53 Martin, John.
3 Martin, John Golrick.
22 Martin, Marcella; Kildare.
8 Martin, Martha; Aughill.
3 Martin, Pat. Golrick.
8 Martin, Rachel; Aughill.
56 Martin, Robert.
61 Martin, Robert.
56 Martin, Thomas.
3 Martin, Thomas.
34 Martin, Thos.; Co. Antrim.
61 Martin, William.
8 Martin, William; Aughill.
30 Martin, William; Markethill.
3 Mason, Daniel.
63 Mason, Thomas & wife.
56 Masterson, Charles.
2 Masterson, Hugh; Granard.
56 Masterson, Patrick.
66 Mathews, Michael; Drogheda.
7 Mathews, Thomas; Dundee.
67 Mathewson, Clark; Strabane.
67 Mathewson, David; Strabane.
62 Maurice, James.
8 Maxwell, Eliza; Rushmills.
33 Maxwell, Isabella; Armagh.
33 Maxwell, James; Armagh.
8 Maxwell, John; Rushmills.
13 Maxwell, Margaret.
8 Maxwell, Margaret; Rushmills.
8 Maxwell, Mrs. T.; Rushmills.
72 Maxwell, Thomas; Kilkenny.
26 Mead, John; Dublin.
13 Mechan, Catherine.
48 Mechan, James.
54 Mechlan, Mary.
54 Mechlan, William.
21 Medile, David.
54 Mein, John; Scotland.
52 Meloy, Jno.
70 Michaw, James.
49 Millar, John.
49 Millar, Robert.
41 Miller, Alexander.
28 Miller, Benjamin; Cothill, Co. Monaghan.
67 Miller, John; Londonderry.
7 Miller, John; Randlestown.

28 Miller, Margaret; Ballybay, Co. Monaghan.
55 Miller, Thomas; Drimkeeran.
49 Miller, William.
16 Millgan, Bernard; Balinahinch.
53 Milliken, W.; Scotland.
32 Minis, Catherine.
28 Minnis, Fras.; Saintfield, Co. Down.
67 Mitchel, James; Letterkenny.
55 Mitchell, Charles.
52 Mitchell, Jas.
69 Mitchell, Martin; Sligo.
68 Mitchell, Samuel; Londonderry.
56 Mite, Samuel.
70 Mochan, Elizabeth.
67 Moffat, Edward; Letterkenny.
19 Moffat, John.
19 Moffat, William.
61 Mollan, Hugh.
22 Molloghan, Patrick; Longford.
3 Molloy, Patrick.
38 Monaghan, Peter; Kings County.
65 Monderson, Isaac; Co. Antrim.
65 Monderson, John; Co. Antrim.
65 Monderson, Margaret; Co. Antrim.
65 Monderson, Sarah; Co. Antrim.
62 Money, Charles.
62 Money, Margaret.
21 Montgomery, John.
29 Moody, James; Armagh.
50 Moone, J.
42 Mooney, Alexander; Co. Antrim.
56 Mooney, John.
42 Mooney, Mary; Co. Antrim.
56 Mooney, Michael.
20 Moore, Alexander; Derry.
45 Moore, Andrew.
16 Moore, James; Donoughmore.
72 Moore, James; Dublin.
20 Moore, Jane; Derry.
19 Moore, John.
28 Moore, John; Belfast.
9 Moore, John; Co. Carlow.
23 Moore, John; Dublin.
20 Moore, Letty; Claugh.
16 Moore, Margaret; Donoughmore.
16 Moore, Robert; Donoughmore.
20 Moore, Samuel; Claugh.
16 Moore, Samuel D.; Carrickfergus.
21 Moore, William.
19 Moore, William.
60 Moore, William; Co. Cavan.
16 Moore, William; Donoughmore.
6 Moran, James.
61 Morer, James.
44 Morgan, Edwd.
5 Morgan, John; Waterford.
66 Morine, John; Kilkenny.
66 Morine, Judith & 2 children; Kilkenny.
1 Morris, John; Boyle, Co. Roscommon.
43 Morris, Mary; Wexford.
50 Morrison. J.
61 Morrison, Matthew.
50 Morrison, R.
33 Morrow, Joseph; Donaghmore, Co. Down.
32 Morrow, Robert.
21 Morrow, Thomas.
25 Morrow, Thos.
40 Morton, Francis; Kilkeel, Co. Down.
60 Muldary, Thomas; Mullingar.
6 Muldawney, Michael.
66 Mulhall, Mary; Kilkenny.
67 Mulheron, John; Letterkenny.
50 Mulholland, Henry.
44 Mulholland, John.

7 Mullan, Arthur; Aghadowy.
48 Mullan, Bridget.
7 Mullan, Cicey; Aghadowy.
33 Mullan, James; Roughforth, Templepatrick.
7 Mullan, John; Aghadowy.
31 Mullan, Richd.; Monaghan.
7 Mullan, William; Aghadowy.
4 Mullay, William; Dublin.
57 Mullen, Edward; Carlow.
57 Mullen, Patrick; Carlow.
57 Mullen, Thomas; Carlow.
65 Mulligan, James C.; Banbridge.
22 Mulligan, Michael; Longford.
57 Mulvany, Patrick; Dublin.
6 Mulvany, Thomas.
56 Mulvey, Isabella.
56 Mulvey, John.
42 Murdoch, John; Co. Down.
4 Murdoch, Obediah; Co. Down.
40 Murney, Patrick; Dublin.
35 Murphy, Bridget; Dublin.
57 Murphy, Bridget; Wexford.
35 Murphy, Catherine; Carlow.
59 Murphy, Cicily; Carlow.
35 Murphy, Dennis; Co. Wexford.
59 Murphy, Eleanor; Carlow.
27 Murphy, Frances.
57 Murphy, Francis; Wexford.
27 Murphy, James.
59 Murphy, James; Carlow.
35 Murphy, James; Dublin.
57 Murphy, Johanna; Wexford.
39 Murphy, John.
1 Murphy, John; Dublin.
9 Murphy, John; Dublin.
57 Murphy, John; Wexford.
57 Murphy, Lawrence; Wexford.
34 Murphy, Marg. & 2 children; Co. Tyrone.
43 Murphy, Martin; Co. Wexford.
57 Murphy, Martin; Wexford.
35 Murphy, Martin; Co. Wexford.
57 Murphy, Mary; Wexford.
35 Murphy, Mary; Co. Wexford.
35 Murphy, Morris; New York.
2 Murphy, Morris; Dublin.
27 Murphy, Patrick.
48 Murphy, Patrick.
21 Murphy, Patrick.
57 Murphy, Simon; Wexford.
43 Murphy, Susan; Co. Wexford.
47 Murray, Bernard.
69 Murray, Bridget; Sligo.
38 Murray, Daniel; Carlow.
61 Murray, James.
24 Murray, Jas.
60 Murray, John, wife & 2 children; Balbriggan.
15 Murray, John; Banbridge.
20 Murray, Patrick; Auchinloe.
34 Murray, William; Co. Armagh.
38 Murray, William; Carlow.
20 Murrin, Thomas; Derry.
2 Murtagh, Mr. & wife; Co. Longford.
66 Murtaugh, John; Westmeath.
69 Murry, Felix; Sligo.

N

36 Nalty, Bridget.
36 Nalty, Margaret.
36 Nalty Mary.
36 Nalty, Patrick.
36 Nalty, Thomas.
22 Narey, Peter; Westmeath.

23 Nasida, Catherine; Dublin.
71 Naughten, Patrick; Athlone, Co. Westmeath.
38 Neal, Michael; Dublin.
8 Neil, James; Ballymoney.
8 Neil, Margaret; Ballymoney.
70 Neill, Henry D.
70 Neill, Madge D.
54 Nesbit, Hugh; Sligo.
38 Nevin, Patrick; Kilkenny.
32 Newberry, Robert.
63 Newlan, Patrick; Co. Carlow.
13 Nickle, Thomas.
48 Nickle, William.
52 Nielson, James.
71 Niven, Patrick; Somerset, Co. Galway.
36 Nolan, P.
50 Noone, John.
63 Nowlan, Charles; Co. Dublin.
15 Nowlan, Christopher; Dublin.
56 Nowland, James.
14 Nugent, Laurence.

O

3 O'Beirn, Michael.
44 O'Boyle, Neal.
29 O'Bream, John; Dublin.
19 O'Brien, John.
60 O'Brien, John, wife, & child; Dublin.
36 O'Brien, Lawrence.
19 O'Brien, Margaret.
36 O'Brien, Mary.
19 O'Brien, Michael.
50 O'Cain, Thos. H.
6 O'Connell, Miss Ann.
60 O'Connor, Thomas; Dublin.
53 O'Donnel, M. & wife.
16 O'Donnell, Isabella; Randlestown.
16 O'Donnell, Mary; Randlestown.
44 O'Donnell, Patk.
5 O'Donnell, Wm. & wife; Waterford.
59 Ogilby, Frederick; Dublin.
59 Ogilby, John; Dublin.
59 Ogilby, Mrs.; Dublin.
59 Ogilby, Robert; Dublin.
26 O'Hara, William; Dublin.
63 O'Hara, William; Tullamore, Kings
County.
41 O'Hare, John.
10 O'Leary, James; Dublin.
50 O'Loone, Henry.
38 O'Neal, Anne.
59 O'Neal, John; Carlow.
38 O'Neal, Nicholas; Dublin.
52 O'Neall, Alexander.
4 O'Neil, Charles; Derry.
50 O'Neil, J.
54 O'Neil, James; Ballymote.
31 O'Neil, John; Rostrevor, Co. Down.
53 O'Neil, John, wife & child.
53 O'Neil, Owen, wife & child.
25 O'Neill, Sarah.
59 O'Reilly, Edward; Carlow.
59 O'Reilly, Eliza; Carlow.
59 O'Reilly, Hugh; Carlow.
59 O'Reilly, Margaret; Carlow.
15 O'Reilly, Miles E.; Dublin.
3 O'Rorke, Bernard.
3 O'Rorke, Patrick.
32 Orr, Anne.
32 Orr, Elizabeth.
32 Orr, George.
32 Orr, James.
32 Orr, Jane.

62 Orr, Patrick.
32 Orr, Thomas.
32 Orr, William
20 Osborne, George; Dromore.
45 O'Shaughnessy, Limerick.
45 O'Shaughnessy, Margaret; Limerick.
20 Owens, James; Armagh.

P

68 Paisley, Christopher; Londonderry.
52 Palmer, Esther.
8 Palmer, Joseph; Magherafelt.
52 Palmer, Margaret.
66 Parcell, Ellen & child; Kilkenny.
45 Park, David.
45 Park, David.
48 Park, Mathew.
31 Parker, John; Dramore, Co. Down.
42 Parker, Moses; Co. Down.
61 Parr, Anne.
61 Parr, Eliza.
61 Parr, John.
61 Parr, Margaret.
61 Parr, Mary.
61 Parr, Thomas.
61 Parr, William.
61 Parr, William, Jun.
13 Patterson, David.
4 Patterson, David; Co. Antrim.
56 Patterson, Edward.
33 Patterson, John; Port Norris.
2 Patterson, Joseph; Co. Cavan.
2 Patterson, William; King's Court, Co.
Cavan.
32 Peacock, James.
48 Peden, James.
28 Peirie, Hugh; Donaghy, Co. Tyrone.
66 Pendergrass, Michael; Kilkenny.
14 Peppard, Patrick & wife.
5 Percival, John; Waterford.
35 Perrin, —; Philadelphia.
43 Pether, William; Co. Wexford.
56 Petit, Berrard.
53 Pettigrew, William.
72 Pettit, Bernard; Co. Longford.
57 Pettit, Patrick; Wexford.
26 Phalen, Daniel; Queens County.
72 Phelan, John; Queens County.
21 Phillips, Bernard.
53 Phoenix, John.
63 Picket, Mark; Co. Carlow.
62 Pierce, Alex.
43 Pierce, John; Co. Wexford.
69 Pigeon, Andrew; Sligo.
15 Pilkington, Edward; Dublin.
22 Pitman, Peter; Nova Scotia.
9 Ploughman, John; Dublin.
72 Pogue, Alexander; Co. Cavan.
62 Poland, Peter.
50 Pole, W.
67 Pollock, John; Londonderry.
49 Pomeroy, James.
22 Poole, Robert; Wexford.
31 Porter, Hugh; wife & 4 children; Dramore, Co. Down.
5 Power, Maurice; Waterford.
35 Prain, Fanny; Philadelphia.
34 Prey, David; Co. Down.
66 Price, Margaret & 3 children; Kilkenny.
66 Priston, William; Leister.
22 Purcel, Charles; Limerick.
22 Purcel, Sarah; Limerick.
22 Purcell, Fanny; Kildare.
2 Purdon, Thomas; Dublin.

Q

55 Queenan, Bryan.
70 Queenan, Martin.
41 Quigley, David.
33 Quin, Agnes; Port Norris, Co. Down.
53 Quin, Arthur.
8 Quin, John; Cookstown.
44 Quince, Thomas.
48 Quinn, Arthur.
68 Quinn, Charles; Donegal.
68 Quinn, Francis; Donegal.
28 Quinn, Henry; Lurgan, Co. Armagh.
68 Quinn, James; Donegal.
68 Quinn, John; Donegal.
37 Quinn, Letita.
13 Quinton, Robert.

R

40 Rafferty, Patrick; Drogheda.
26 Rafferty, Simeon; Dublin.
53 Rafferty, Stewart.
72 Rafter, Dennis; Kilkenny.
71 Raftrey, John; Athlone, Co. Westmeath.
27 Ragan, T.
8 Rainey, James; Ballymena.
20 Ramsey, George; Coleraine.
48 Rankin, Sarah.
33 Rea, Patrick.
29 Read, James; Dublin.
47 Read, Thomas.
37 Recard, George.
5 Recard, John & wife; Waterford.
22 Rechil, Patrick; Longford.
71 Reddington, Patrick; Loughrea, Co.
   Galway.
33 Reed, John.
62 Reed, Martin.
71 Regin, John; St. Nicholas, Galway.
31 Reid, Adam; Clare, Co. Armagh.
50 Reid, George.
50 Reid, James.
8 Reid, James; Ballymena.
50 Reid, M.
50 Reid, Rachael.
50 Reid, Robert.
50 Reid, Thomas.
1 Reilly. —; Shercock, Co. Cavan.
59 Reilly, Charles; Meath.
1 Reilly, Fras; Granard.
2 Reilly, John; King's Court, Co. Cavan.
1 Reilly, Michael; Cavan.
9 Reilly, Patrick; Co. Longford.
38 Reilly, Thomas.
59 Reilly, Thomas; Meath.
14 Reily, Philip.
48 Renenaugh, James.
41 Reynolds, Catherine.
56 Reynolds, Eliza.
56 Reynolds, Joseph.
56 Reynolds, Laurence.
55 Reynolds, Patrick.
63 Reynolds, William; Co. Kildare.
35 Riall, Patrick; Dublin.
31 Rice, Canlan; Ballybay, Co. Monaghan.
33 Rice, Patrick; Camlagh, Co. Armagh.
68 Richie, Catherine; Tyrone.
68 Richie, William; Tyrone.
70 Richley, Daniel.
62 Riddle, Samuel.
62 Riddle, William.
71 Rider, William; Aghram, Co. Galway.
48 Ridge, James.
51 Rielly, Eliza.
51 Rielly, Elizabeth.
51 Rielly, Rose.
27 Riordan, Coleman.
62 Ritchie, John.
62 Ritchie, Wm.
70 Roaney, Anne.
70 Roany, Charles.
65 Robb, Charles; Philadelphia.
34 Roberts, John M.; Co. Antrim.
39 Robertson, Catharine.
44 Robertson, D.
44 Robertson, Eleanor.
8 Robin, William; Banbridge.
66 Robins, Bridget & child; Westmeath.
44 Robinson, John.
8 Robinson, John; Newtownards.
8 Robinson, Joseph; Co. Cavan.
68 Robinson, Thomas; Antrim.
11 Robinson, Mrs. & family; Ireland.
43 Roche, David; Co. Wexford.
27 Roche, James.
43 Roche, John; Co. Wexford.
27 Roche, William.
43 Rochford, Francis; Co. Wexford.
57 Rochford, Walter; Wexford.
13 Rodgers, Patrick.
47 Rogan, Charles.
62 Rogers, Alexr.
62 Rogers, Ann.
61 Rogers, Hugh.
48 Rogers, John.
16 Rogers, John; Ballinahinch.
62 Rogers, John & wife.
62 Rogers, Mary.
28 Rogers, Patrick; Derry.
70 Roney, Catherine.
28 Rooney, Hugh; Malenadony, Co. Leitrim.
54 Rooney, Michael.
55 Rooney, Michael.
69 Roony, Charles; Sligo.
54 Roony, John; Tauly.
54 Roony, Sarah; Tauly.
68 Rosborough, John; Londonderry.
24 Rose, Geo.
70 Rosman, Martin.
61 Ross, James.
60 Roundtree, Owen & wife; Dublin.
46 Rowan, James; Belfast.
43 Rowan, John; Mountrath.
53 Rowan, Mary & 4 children.
43 Rowan, Margaret; Mountrath.
2 Rowland, Mrs. & child.
66 Rudd, Grace; Dublin.
62 Ruddock, James.
14 Russel, Isaac.
46 Russell, Alexander; Donegal.
46 Russell, Francis; Donegal.
46 Russell, James; Donegal.
46 Russell, Jane; Donegal.
44 Russell, John.
46 Russell, John; Donegal.
50 Rutledge, John.
19 Ryan, Ellen.
19 Ryan, James.
66 Ryan, Margaret; Carlow.
66 Ryan, Mary & child; Carlow.

S

66 Salmon, Mathew; Meath.
15 Salter, Thomas; Dublin.
7 Sampson, David; Dundee.
31 Sampson, John; Ballygalley, Co. Tyrone.
40 Saunderson, Henry; Portadown, Co.
   Armagh.
69 Scandler, Bryan; Sligo.
67 Scanlon, Maney; Letterkenny.

4 Scellan, Thos.; Dublin.	42 Sloan, Catherine; Co. Antrim.
61 Scilly, Jane.	61 Sloan, James.
61 Scilly, John.	16 Sloan, William; Armagh.
61 Scilly, Margaret.	56 Smith, —.
69 Scinlon, Bryan; Castleton.	56 Smith, —.
13 Scott, Catherine.	8 Smith, Abraham; Co. Antrim.
48 Scott, Edward.	54 Smith, Alexander; Scotland.
61 Scott, Eliza.	2 Smith, Bernard; Cavan.
13 Scott, Hugh.	56 Smith, Catharine.
13 Scott, Jane.	48 Smith, Eliza.
61 Scott, Jane.	8 Smith, Hugh; Co. Antrim.
44 Scott, John.	65 Smith, Hugh; Co. Antrim.
44 Scott, John.	62 Smith, James.
61 Scott, Sarah.	48 Smith, John.
65 Scott, Thomas W.; Philadelphia.	2 Smith, John; England.
54 Scott, Walter; Scotland.	7 Smith, Joseph; Drimaragh.
13 Scott, William.	14 Smith, Michael.
35 Sculler, James; Co. Wexford.	6 Smith, Peter.
39 Seeds, William.	70 Smith, Peter.
68 Segarson, William; Londonderry.	14 Smith, Phillip.
68 Semple, Robert; Londonderry.	35 Smith, Robert; Dublin.
7 Semple, Thomas; Aghadowy.	2 Smith, Thomas; Jun.; Cavan.
42 Service, Alexander; Co. Antrim.	2 Smith, Thos. & wife; Co. Cavan.
1 Shales, —; Shercock, Co. Cavan.	42 Smyth, Jane; Co. Down.
16 Shanks, William & wife; Dromore.	19 Smyth, John.
48 Shannan, John.	56 Smyth, Patrick.
8 Shannon, David; Drumbo.	20 Smyth, Robert; Dromore.
7 Shannon, Hugh & wife; Belfast.	67 Smyth, Robert; Enniskillen.
50 Shannon, M.	13 Smyth, William.
4 Shannon, Quinton; Co. Down.	47 Somerville, Jane.
68 Sharkey, William; Donegal.	47 Somerville, Mary.
37 Sharkey, William & sister.	8 Spark, James; Derrock.
52 Shaw, Ann.	53 Sparks, Alexander; Scotland.
52 Shaw, James.	53 Sparks, Eliza; Scotland.
52 Shaw, John.	22 Spelman, D.; Longford.
8 Shaw, John; Co. Antrim.	8 Spencer, Robert; Co. Antrim.
52 Shaw, Mary.	44 Spencer, Samuel.
52 Shaw, Robert.	5 Spratt, Andrew; Waterford.
52 Shaw, Rose.	42 Spratt, Mary; Co. Down.
52 Shaw, Rose.	42 Spratt, Thomas; Co. Down.
52 Shaw, Thomas.	68 Spraule, Armour; Tyrone.
52 Shaw, Wm.	14 Spunner, Thomas.
48 Shearer, Mathew.	55 Standford, Edward.
27 Sheehey, Mary.	23 Stanley, Peter; Dublin.
42 Shepherd, Jane; Co. Tyrone.	51 Stasey, Doritha.
42 Shepherd, Margaret; Co. Armagh.	51 Stasey, Eliza.
42 Shepherd, Richard; Co. Armagh.	51 Stasey, John.
42 Shepherd, Simpson; Co. Derry.	51 Stasey, Margaret.
14 Sheppard, James & wife.	51 Stasey, Sarah.
14 Sheppard, Peter & wife.	51 Stasey, Wm.
68 Sheran. Andrew; Tyrone.	23 Stavely, Andrew; Antrim.
2 Sherdon, Jane; Killeshandra.	16 Steel, James; Larne.
2 Sherdon, Thomas; Killeshandra.	4 Steel, William; Co. Antrim.
38 Sherlock, Robert.	3 Steen, Robert; Co. Antrim.
18ª Shields, Frindley; Ireland.	3 Stephens, John.
45 Shields, William Junr.	48 Stephens, John.
45 Shields, William Senr.	72 Stephens, John; Dublin.
49 Simpson, —.	16 Sterling, Sobert; Derry.
61 Simpson, James.	69 Stevens, James; Sligo.
49 Simpson, Robert.	57 Stevens, William; Wexford.
62 Simpson, Wm. & wife.	22 Steward, Geo.; Monaghan.
50 Singer, James.	52 Stewart, Alexander.
43 Sinnot, Richard; Wexford.	8 Stewart, Alexander; Belfast.
20 Sinton, Henry; Bushill.	16 Stewart, Alexander; Drumbridge.
20 Sinton, James; Bushill.	62 Stewart, Allan.
20 Sinton, John; Bushill.	8 Stewart, Charles; Rushmills.
20 Sinton, Joseph; Bushill.	61 Stewart, Daniel.
20 Sinton, Rebecca; Bushill.	48 Stewart, David.
68 Sithgon, William; Londonderry.	8 Stewart, James; Rushmills.
22 Slattery, Patrick; Tipperary.	52 Stewart, Jane.
19 Slavin, Anne.	62 Stewart, Jane.
19 Slavin, Catherine.	62 Stewart, John.
19 Slavin, James.	8 Stewart, John; Rushmills.
19 Slavin, Michael.	62 Stewart, John & wife.
32 Sleith, John.	8 Stewart, Mrs. Letitia; Belfast.
32 Sleith, Margaret.	52 Stewart, Martha.
61 Slinler, M.	8 Stewart, Rebecca; Belfast.
42 Sloan, Catherine; Co. Antrim.	52 Stewart, Robert.

8 Stewart, Rose; Rushmills.
8 Stewart, Sally; Rushmills.
49 Stewart, Samuel.
13 Stewart, Thomas.
48 Stewart, William.
52 Stewart, Wm.
42 Stilt, John; Co. Armagh.
1 Stinton, Daniel; City of Limerick.
13 Stoop, John.
48 Story, Robert.
22 Stram, John; Fernagh.
48 Strawbridge, John.
23 Strean, John; Newtownards.
33 Stuart, James; Hill-Hall, Co. Down.
68 Stuart, William; Londonderry.
68 Stuart, William; Tyrone.
27 Sullivan, Jeremiah.
52 Swan, Alexander.
52 Swan, David.
52 Swan, John.
52 Swan, Margaret.
52 Swan, Margaret.
63 Sweeney, Terence.
63 Sweeney, Terence.
20 Sweeny, Andrew; Burligh.
20 Sweeny, Anne; Burligh.
20 Sweeny, Archibald; Burligh.
61 Sweeny, Catherine.
61 Sweeny, Eleanor.
34 Sweeny, James; Co. Antrim.
54 Sweeny, Jeremiah; Coolerrah.
20 Sweeny, Mary; Burligh.
20 Sweeny, William; Burligh.
66 Sweetman, Catharine; Meath.

T

62 Taggart, William & wife.
53 Tanner, John.
23 Taylor, Michael; Perth, Scotland.
55 Taylor, Richard; Sligo.
15 Templeton, William; Belfast.
61 Temen, Robert.
59 Thomas, William; Wexford.
7 Thompson, Andrew; New York.
3 Thompson, Mr.
40 Thompson, Arthur; Liverpool.
23 Thompson, Geo.; Antrim.
59 Thompson, George; Dublin.
62 Thompson, James.
71 Thompson, James; Stonepark, Co. Roscommon.
21 Thompson, John.
49 Thompson, John.
13 Thompson, Joseph.
8 Thompson, Mary; Dromore.
53 Thompson, Thomas.
8 Thompson, Thomas; Dromore.
49 Thompson, William.
48 Thompson, William.
20 Thornberry, Susan; Bushill.
57 Thornton, John; Dundalk.
57 Thornton, Nicholas; Dundalk.
57 Tierney, Francis; Carlow.
57 Tierney, Joseph; Carlow.
57 Tierney, Margaret; Carlow.
46 Tierny, Hugh; Donegal.
29 Tighe, Michael; Co. Antrim.
44 Tigut, Matthew.
50 Tiney, Thomas.
15 Tindall, William; Dublin.
5 Tobin, Catherine; Waterford.
61 Todd, Samuel.
13 Todd, Stephen.
45 Toland, John.
39 Toner, B.
38 Tonnaly, James; Co. Meath.
71 Toole, Michael; Tram, Co. Galway.

49 Todd, Thomas.
62 Tone, Robert.
6 Tracey, William.
72 Tracy, Catharine; Kilkenny.
72 Tracy, Dennis; Kilkenny:
72 Tracy, Mary; Kilkenny.
72 Tracy, Thomas; Kilkenny.
69 Travers, Patrick; Lurganboy.
70 Trotter, William.
40 Trotter, William; Monmouth, New Jersey.
42 Turley, Anne; Co. Down.
42 Turley, Eliza; Co. Down.
42 Turley, John; Co. Down.
42 Turley, Sarah; Co. Down.
42 Turley, Sarah; Co. Down.
59 Twamley, George; Wicklow.
59 Twamley, Jane; Wicklow.
59 Twamley, Mary; Wicklow.

V

60 Vaharty, Miles; Enniscorthy.
27 Vaughan, James.
27 Vaughan, Thomas.
27 Vaughan, Y.
19 Veatch, James.

W

63 Wacum, Robert, wife & child; Co. Dublin.
43 Wade, James & wife; Dublin.
60 Waldron, Thomas; Balbriggan.
48 Walker, Constantine.
61 Walker, David.
61 Walker, David.
48 Walker, Eliza.
48 Walker, George.
50 Walker, H.
50 Walker, J.
50 Walker, J.
48 Walker, James.
61 Walker, Jane.
16 Walker, John F.; Rich Hill.
48 Walker, Joseph.
50 Walker, M.
61 Walker, Martha.
48 Walker, Mary.
50 Walker, R.
48 Walker, William.
68 Walker, William; Londonderry.
4 Walkinshaw, William; Co. Antrim.
20 Wallace, Hannah; Dromore.
41 Wallace, James.
62 Wallace, Margaret.
53 Wallace, S.
20 Wallace, Thomas; Dromore.
19 Walsh, Bridget.
27 Walsh, Daniel.
19 Walsh, Eliza.
2 Walsh, Hugh; Co. Tipperary.
43 Walsh, James; Co. Wexford.
62 Walsh, John.
38 Walsh, John; Tipperary.
2 Walsh, Lawrence; Co. Tipperary.
22 Walsh, M. R.; Sligo.
1 Walsh, Patrick; Dublin.
48 Wantya, Richmond.
70 Ward, Anne.
70 Ward, Patrick.
26 Ward, William; Carlow.
43 Wardle, Jeremiah; Lancashire.
68 Wardler, Hugh; Tyrone.
13 Ware, James.
50 Warnick, R.
23 Warnock, John; Dublin.

59 Warr, Eliza; England.
59 Warr, George; England.
59 Warr, Samuel; England.
63 Warren, Edward; Co. Carlow.
63 Warren, John; Co. Carlow.
51 Warrier, George.
66 Wass, John; Dublin.
65 Waters, Archibald; Co. Antrim.
55 Waters, John.
55 Waters, Roger.
3 Waters, Winifred.
63 Waters, —; City of Dublin.
15 Waterson, John; Belfast.
61 Watson, Alexander.
28 Watson, James; Newtownards; Co. Down.
8 Watson, William; Co. Tyrone.
67 Watt, James; Templemore.
30 Watts, Charles; Tyrone.
30 Watts, James; Tyrone.
30 Watts, Jane; Tyrone.
30 Watts, Joseph; Tyrone.
30 Watts, Margaret; Tyrone.
30 Watts, Mary; Tyrone.
42 Weathers, Joseph; Co. Down.
4 Webster, Thomas; England.
51 Weeks, Caroline.
14 Weeks, Charles.
51 Weeks, Frances.
51 Weeks, Jane.
51 Weeks, Thos.
5 Wells, Peter; Waterford.
55 West, Anne.
24 West, Jas.
51 West, John.
51 West, Margaret.
51 West, Margaret.
14 West, Thmoas.
55 West, William.
51 West, Wm.
26 Whalen, Thomas; Dublin.
22 Wheelock, Alice; Wexford.
2 Whelan, Nicholas.
5 Whelan, Patrick; Waterford.
5 Whit, John; Waterford.
68 White, Alexander; Tyrone.
68 White, Elizabeth; Tyrone.
68 White, Ellen; Tyrone.
59 White, Francis; Dublin.
70 White, James.
48 White, Jane.
22 White, Richard; Dublin.
68 White, Mathew; Tyrone.
45 Whiteside, William.
34 Whitford, William; Co. Antrim.
30 Wigging, Rachel; Monaghan.
61 Wiggins, Henry.
47 Wiley, Ann.
47 Wiley, Elizabeth.
45 Wiley, John.

47 Wiley, Mary.
47 Wiley, Thomas.
27 Wilis, James.
3 Wilkinson, John.
3 Wilkinson, William.
32 Willes, Joshua.
32 Willes, Mary.
26 William, Mrs. E. W.; Dublin.
27 Willis, Eleanor.
27 Willis, Richard.
30 Wilson, Rev. A.; Jonesborough.
56 Wilson, Charles.
65 Wilson, David; Co. Tyrone.
4 Wilson, James; Co. Antrim.
42 Wilson, James; Co. Armagh.
65 Wilson, James; Co. Tyrone.
70 Wilson, Jane.
13 Wilson, John.
65 Wilson, Joseph; Co. Tyrone.
45 Wilson, Marcus.
65 Wilson, Mary; Co. Tyrone.
62 Wilson, Matthew.
61 Wilson, Robert.
42 Wilson, Sarah; Co. Armagh.
53 Wilson, Thomas.
14 Wilson, Thomas.
12 Wilson, Thomas; Dublin.
29 Wilson, William; Co. Antrim.
43 Winstanley, John; Dublin.
15 Withers, Wm.; Belfast.
20 Wood, Thomas; Auchnalcoy.
61 Woods, Eliza.
61 Woods, James.
8 Woods, Ruth; Richhill.
8 Woods, William; Richhill.
50 Woodside, R.
50 Woodside, Wm.
28 Workman, George; Tamletocrilly, Co. Derry.
68 Worrhington, John; Londonderry.
13 Wray, James.
13 Wray, William.
39 Wright, Henry.
69 Wright, James; Newtown Stewart.
69 Wright, Jane; Sligo.
69 Wright, John; Sligo.
69 Wright, Mariam; Sligo.
32 Wright, Mathan.
21 Wright, Michael.
13 Wright, William.
54 Wynne, Patrick.

Y

55 Young, Alexander.
55 Young, Eliza & child.
62 Young, John.
55 Young, Robert.
68 Young, Susan; Londonderry.
55 Young, Thomas; Drimkeeran.

LIST OF SHIPS
ARRIVING IN AMERICAN PORTS, 1815 AND 1816.

Code No.	Port of Departure	Date of Arrival 1815	Name of Ship	Port of Entry	Passengers	Point of Origin
1	Dublin	......	Nautilus	New York	18	County
2	Dublin	......	Amphion	New York	48	County
3	Sligo	......	Helen	New York	38	......
4	Belfast	Sept. 2	Christopher	New York	37	County
5	Waterford	Sept. 2	Virginia	New York	33	County
6	Dublin	Sept. 24	Mary	New York	23	......
7	Belfast	Oct. 14	George	New York	53	County
8	Belfast	Oct. 26	James Bayley	New York	98	County
9	Dublin	Nov. 10	C. Fawcett	New York	23	County
10	Liverpool	Nov. 14	William	New York	2	County
11	Halifax	Nov. 14	Two Friends	New York	3	County
12	Liverpool	Nov. 14	Mexico	New York	4	......
13	Londonderry	Nov. 14	Marcus Hill	New York	121	County
14	Dublin	Oct. 23	George & Albert	Philadelphia	42	County
15	Dublin	Nov. 18	Orient	New York	35	County
16	Belfast	Nov. 22	Westpoint	New York	47	County
17	Liverpool	......	Minerva	New York	5	......
18	Lisbon	......	Courier	New York	4	......
18a	Demarara	......	Favorite	New York	1	......
19	Dublin	Nov. 24	Sally	New York	57	County
20	Londonderry	Nov. 25	Emp. Alexander	New York	64	......
21	Newry	......	Leda	New York	22	......

1816

Code No.	Port of Departure	Date of Arrival	Name of Ship	Port of Entry	Passengers	Point of Origin
22	Dublin	Jan. 19	Ontario	New York	56	County
23	Belfast	Jan. 18	Shannon	New York	32	County
24	Dublin	Mar. 11	Erin	New York	31	......
25	Dublin	Mar. 7	Amphion	New York	20	County
26	Dublin	Apr. 3	Dublin Packet	New York	39	County
27	Cork	Apr. 13	Anne	New York	34	County
28	Belfast	May 2	Lorenzo	New York	53	......
29	Dublin	Apr. 25	Hannah	Philadelphia	15	County
30	Newry	May 4	Nancy	Baltimore	22	County
31	Newry	May 4	Globe	New York	23	County
32	Belfast	May 5	Elizabeth	New York	46	......

LIST OF SHIPS—Continued

Code No.	Port of Departure	Date of Arrival 1816	Port of Entry	Name of Ship	Passengers	Point of Origin
33	Newry	May 6	Philadelphia	Dido	22	County
34	Belfast	May 10	New York	John	18	County
35	Dublin	May 12	New York	Ch. Fawcett	31	County
36	Galway	May 12	New York	Hare	30	....
37	Londonderry	May 13	Philadelphia	Active	25	....
38	Dublin	May 17	Philadelphia	Louisa	26	County
39	Newry	....	New York	Aeolus	36	....
40	Londonderry	Jun. 4	New York	London	24	County
41	Newry	Jun. 4	New York	Foster	50	....
42	Belfast	Jun. 5	New York	Westpoint	45	County
43	Dublin	Jun. 1	New York	Wilson	37	County
44	Londonderry	Jun. 10	New York	Enterprize	33	....
45	Londonderry	....	Philadelphia	Falcon	34	....
46	Londonderry	Jun. 14	New York	Jane	33	County
47	Belfast	Jun. 15	New York	William Hill	20	County
48	Londonderry	Jun. 15	New York	Marcus	155	County
49	Londonderry	Jun. 17	New York	Niagara	34	County
50	Belfast	Jun. 20	New York	Ossian	90	....
51	Dublin	Jun. 22	Philadelphia	Conistoga	45	....
52	Belfast	Jun. 24	Philadelphia	George	46	....
53	Belfast	Jun. 26	New York	Sophia	82	....
54	Sligo	Jun. 30	New York	Foundling	90	Place
55	Sligo	Jly. 1	New York	Orient	57	County
56	Dublin	Jly. 1	Philadelphia	Bristol	47	....
57	Dublin	Jly. 2	New York	Ceres	37	County
58	Halifax	....	New York	Montague	2	County
59	Dublin	Jly. 3	New York	Dibby & Eliza	64	County
60	Dublin	Jly. 6	Philadelphia	Only Son	29	County
61	Belfast	Jly. 8	New York	George of Brazil	91	....
62	Dublin	Jly. 15	New York	Prince of Brazil	99	....
63	Dublin	Jly. 10	New London	Actress	31	Place
64	Newry	Aug. 1	Philadelphia	Boudain	37	County
65	Belfast	Jly. 22	New York	Alpha	46	Place
66	Dublin	Aug. 1	New York	Ontario	97	County
67	Londonderry	Aug. 14	New York	Barkley	58	Place
68	Londonderry	Aug. 12	New York	Mount-Bay	133	County
69	Sligo	Aug. 16	New York	Juno	38	County
70	Sligo	Aug. 8	New York	Margaret	54	....
71	Galway	Aug. 2	New York	John	40	Place
72	Dublin	Aug. 14	New York	Bristol	40	Place